P9-CDO-305

*Who can find a virtuous woman?*
*for her price is far above rubies.*
*Her children arise up, and call her blessed;*
*her husband also, and he praiseth her.*

*Prov. 31: 10, 28*

# WOMEN OF TEXAS

*Introduction by*

**Mrs. John Connally**

*Oil Paintings by*

**John French**

**James M. Day**
**Billy M. Jones**
**Dayton Kelley**
**W.C. Nunn**
**Rupert N. Richardson**
**Harold B. Simpson**
**Martha Anne Turner**
**Dorman H. Winfrey**

TEXIAN PRESS 1972 WACO, TEXAS



Howard County Library
Big Spring, Texas

First Edition

Published by

Waco, Texas

Bound by
Library Binding Co.
Waco, Texas

Dedicated To

The Women of Texas

# Introduction

Texas had traditionally considered herself part of the South. From the beginnings of Anglo-American colonization, a high percentage of immigrants to Texas have come from the southern United States. With them they brought a rich and complex cultural heritage.

Perhaps the strongest element in this heritage and that most deeply rooted in the hearts of Southerners, was the ideal of the southern gentleman — independent, self-assured, brave, and courteous. Complementing it of course, was the southern lady — paragon of domestic virtue. She was at the opposite pole from her masculine counterpart — in the words of one southern novelist writing in 1836, "tis man's to act, 'tis woman's to endure." It was acknowledged by all, man and woman alike, that women were to "content themselves with their humble household duties." The grip of this conviction predetermined that there would be no women governors, no women writers, no women artists.

Yet there were. In spite of poor schooling, in spite of the scorn of family and neighbors, in spite of the day long chores demanded of them, women did distinguish themselves. From the earliest days of immigration across the Sabine and Red River, women played a role in charting the course of history in Texas.

Not all the ways in which women have contributed to the history of the Lone Star State have defied the cultural tradition — indeed, as a group their greatest contribution has been in that very role assigned them, in which they freed man from all the small tasks of day-to-day existence, that he might spend his days building empires and creating noble works of art and thought. But if the contribution of woman has almost solely been anonymous and non-individualized, women have made unique contributions and their names have been remembered. Among these are the women commemorated in *Women of Texas*.

There are four ways in which women have made individual contributions to the history of Texas, or indeed, to the history of the human race. Each of these is found in the lives of the women in this book. Covering the entire course of Texas history from Mexican statehood to the twentieth century, *Women of Texas* demonstrates the continuous role played by women in our state's history.

The contributions women have made, with the most representatives, encompasses those women who are remembered chiefly as symbolic figures. In this volume they are represented by Jane Long, "Mother of Texas", and Margaret Moffett Lea Houston, pre-eminent in all the best qualities demanded of a first lady of the Republic.

Likewise, the second kind of contribution of women to our history depends not on individual action, but on circumstances of time and place. Under this category are women remembered as figures in the historical drama who were objects of action, rather than its movers. Nonetheless, they are central figures in events which mark major episodes in our history. Such women are depicted here in the persons of Cynthia Ann Parker and Mrs. Almaron Dickinson.

Third are women whose actions do not merely confirm the course of events, but determine them, but who nonetheless act for their husbands or other men and not in their own right. Such women have frequently been powerful behind the throne, or even on it, but have achieved their place through another's merits. Mrs. James Ferguson, one of only three women state governors in the history of the United States, was such a woman. As she and her husband admitted freely in her campaign, her husband not she would be the real governor after her election.

Finally, these are women who have achieved recognition for achievements based on their own talent, initiative, courage, or genius. Women with these qualities, are rare and exceptional individuals. Perhaps a large part of the explanation for Texas' astounding history lies in the extraordinary number of such figures whose lives have touched the state. In this volume three such persons are sketched: Mary Austin Holley, Elisabet Ney, and Mollie Bailey. All three lived vigorous and productive lives, and the things for which they are remembered were created out of their own efforts. Mollie Bailey was a spy for the Confederate army, a nurse, an entertainer, and an entrepreneur who created and operated one of the country's largest circuses. Mary Austin Holley devoted her literary skills to describing life in the Republic of Texas, and her letters and books, published in the East, did much to bring the young Republic sympathy and aid and to encourage its settlement. Elisabet Ney, an extra-ordinary person, was already a sculptor of international renown when she chose to settle in Texas. She made a major contribution to Texas when she offered her talents to portray some of its outstanding leaders.

The women portrayed in this volume are representative of all the various ways in which women have molded the growth of our State. Their stories are a fitting addition to the Texian Press series of works on selected topics of Texas' history. Again a panel of distinguished names in Texas history has joined to present a vivid portrayal of one of the many fascinating aspects of the State's past. I have watched this series grow not only with pleasure that the story of our state is being so well presented, but with a certain personal pride that Governor Connally and I might have helped in a small way to inspire the renewal of interest in Texas' past, to which this volume is a tribute.

I commend these ladies of the past and have much confidence in the contribution to be made by Texas ladies of today and of the future.

Nellie Connally

Mrs. John Connally

# John French

John French, a native of Waco, is one of the fastest rising young artists in Texas. Born on January 10, 1936, he spent most of his earlier years in Central Texas where he graduated from Waco Technical High School. During the next few years he worked in west and south Texas and in New Mexico and served four years in the United States Air Force as an aircraft hydraulics systems specialist. Returning to Waco, he worked as a mechanic for twelve years.

During all this time he painted at night and in his spare time, beginning as a small boy using colored chalk, pencils, and "whatever was available." His wide travel and keen observation has given him a deep appreciation for early Texas architecture, landscapes, wild life and western scenes.

Although he had never had formal art training, he left his job as a mechanic in June of 1971 and began painting full time. Since then his paintings have increased in popularity and are acclaimed by noted art critics and collectors all over Texas and the Southwest. Many of his works are now in private collections and have been exhibited in several Texas cities, Denver, Tucson, Honolulu, and Tokyo, Japan.

Much of the research for his paintings is done by his wife, the former Wanda Burns of Waco. She is an omnivorous reader and as she reads, she picks out facts and information in which her artist husband would be interested or would need to know in order to make his paintings historically accurate.

For the paintings in this book, both John and Wanda researched the subjects in the Texas Collection at Baylor University, the Waco-McLennan County Library, the Elisabet Ney Studio in Austin, and the Texas State Archives.

The Frenchs make their home at 2500 Stewart Drive in Waco.

## The Paintings

*Jane Long*

Often referred to as the "Mother of Texas," Jane Long was the first known woman of English descent to come to Texas. In 1821 she spent the winter in a rude fort on Bolivar peninsular near present Galveston while her husband, Dr. James Long, was on an expedition into the interior. Mrs. Long's only companions during that time were a daughter, a servant, and a second daughter born on December 21, 1821. The baby, Mary Long, was the first known child of English ancestry born in Texas. The painting in this book depicts the privations endured by Mrs. Long and her companions during the severe winter.

*Mary Austin Holley*

Mary Austin Holley, a cousin to the Father of Texas, Stephen F. Austin, was a prodigious traveller and spent much time in Texas. The author of one of the earliest books about Texas, she is shown in the painting leaving the river boat which has brought her up the Brazos River to a landing near the home of her cousin at Peach Point.

*Suzanna Dickinson*

Suzanna Dickinson, who survived the massacre of the Texans in the Alamo in 1836, is one of the best known of all Texas heroines. The artist has captured that poignant moment in the drama as she was being led from her place of concealment during the battle to an audience with General Santa Anna. The "Babe of the Alamo," little Angelina Dickinson, is in her mother's arms and all around is the carnage, wrought by both Texans and Mexicans on that March 6, the day the Alamo fell.

*Cynthia Ann Parker*

Captured by the Indians when she was a small girl, Cynthia Ann Parker grew up and married a Comanche chief, Peta Nocona, by whom she had several children. Two of these appear in the painting. They are Prairie Flower, the youngest, and Quanah, who later became chief of the tribe. Peta Nocona also appears in the painting, which recreates a typical camp scene just prior to Cynthia Ann's recapture by a group of Texans in 1860.

*Margaret Lea Houston*

Twenty-year-old Margaret Moffett Lea first met Sam Houston at the home of her brother in Mobile, Alabama in May of 1839. Although Houston was twenty-six years her senior, by the time he left Mobile a few days later to return to Texas, she had promised to become his wife. The painting in this book captures the farewell scene between the two.

*Elisabet Ney*

Elisabet Ney was the first eminent Texas sculptor and in her studio created several outstanding pieces of work. In the painting in this book, Miss Ney is shown working on the bust of Governor Joseph W. Sayers in her Austin studio.

*Mollie Bailey*

Mollie Bailey, the circus queen of Texas during the years immediately following the Civil War, is depicted in a typical circus scene. Here amid the animal cages, the gaily painted wagons and the carnival atmosphere of the big top, Mrs. Bailey liked to greet the crowds who came from near and far when the circus came to town. Her husband Gus had served in the Confederate Army and the Baileys were said to have admitted free all Confederate veterans who came to see their show.

*Miriam A. Ferguson*

Miriam A. (Ma) Ferguson, the only woman ever to serve as governor of Texas and one of the first in the nation, is pictured in front of the Governor's Mansion in Austin. Several changes have since been made in the appearance of the mansion, but it appears here as it looked during Mrs. Ferguson's term of office and her occupancy of the house.

Dayton Kelley
Texas Collection
Baylor University

# Table of Contents


Jane Wilkinson Long .................................... Page 5

Mary Austin Holley .................................... Page 35

Suzanna Dickinson .................................... Page 59

Cynthia Ann Parker .................................... Page 73

Margaret Moffette Lea Houston ............ Page 95

Elisabet Ney .................................... Page 119

Mollie Bailey .................................... Page 137

Miriam Amanda Ferguson ...................... Page 157

# Jane Wilkinson Long

JANE LONG

# Jane Wilkinson Long

by
MARTHA ANNE TURNER

Jane Wilkinson Long occupies a unique role in Texas history. The equal of Sam Houston and sometimes acclaimed as the feminine counterpart of David Crockett and "the Mother of Texas," Mrs. Long was eminently more. Just as her distinguished forebears contributed to the history of the United States from its genesis in 1776 to its expansion to the Pacific, so did Jane Wilkinson Long pursue a fearless course of destiny that began in 1819, continued through the Americanization of Texas and the Civil War, and ended only with her death in 1880.

The seventh daughter and tenth child of Captain Mackall Wilkinson and Anne Herbert (Dent) Wilkinson, Mrs. Long was born at Truman Place Plantation in Charles County, Maryland, July 23, 1798. In conformity with family tradition, she was christened Jane Herbert Wilkinson in honor of her maternal grandmother. Sometimes identified as "the Daughter of Maryland" because of her birth in that state, Jane Long was descended from illustrious forebears. On her father's side there were two distinct lines of Wilkinsons. In Jane's direct paternal line was the Honorable William Wilkinson, Sr., an Englishman and her father's great grandfather, who settled in the province of Maryland in the middle of the seventeenth century. The founder of the strain was of the landed gentry, a man of affairs, a prominent businessman, and a public official. William Mackall Wilkinson, who had served as a captain in the Revolutionary War, was the son of William Wilkinson, II, and the grandson of Francis Wilkinson. The other Wilkinson line was that of Captain Joseph Wilkinson, whose son Joseph was the paternal grandfather of General James Wilkinson. The latter, who was born near Benedict, in Tidewater, Maryland, in 1757, is often erroneously referred to as William Mackall's brother and Jane's uncle. Of this strain, the first Joseph Wilkinson emigrated to the United States from England in 1729. An affluent planter of Calvert County, Maryland, James Wilkinson's father, whose estate was located on a peninsula formed by the Patuxent and Potomac rivers, was a man of considerable moral stature who had his children educated by private tutors.

Jane's forefathers on her maternal side were equally distinguished. General John Dent, her grandfather on the distaff side, was an outstanding officer in the Revolutionary War and a close friend of General George Washington. General Dent held civil honors as well as those in the military.

Jane's mother was said to have been close to her celebrated father and relied on his wise counsel, especially after she became widowed. Jane's father died in Charles County, March 12, 1799, at the age of 47, the year following his daughter's birth.

The Honorable George Dent, one of Jane's uncles on her mother's side, was also an officer of the Revolutionary War and a statesman of distinction. Dent held several important elective positions including the speakership of the Lower House and of the Assembly and later the presidency of the State Senate of Maryland. Elected to the third, fourth, fifth, and sixth Congresses as a Democrat — from March 4, 1793 to March 3, 1801 — he also served as speaker pro tempore of that body. During his last term in the Senate, George Dent was influential in the election of his close friend Thomas Jefferson to the presidency of the United States.

One of the Senator's sons, John Herbert Dent was the famous officer of the United States Navy who was midshipman on the *Constellation* when it defeated the *Insurgente* in 1799. Another in the distaff line, Captain Thomas Marshall Dent was the maternal grandfather of General James Longstreet, a Confederate officer of the Civil War. Still another in the line, Miss Julia Dent, the daughter of the unreconstructed rebel Frederick Dent of Missouri and distant relative of Longstreet, married General Ulysses S. Grant in 1848 and graced the White House in Washington, D. C. as first lady from 1869 to 1877. In the marriage of Miss Anna Longstreet, sister of the Confederate general, to Dr. Hutchinson Dent, two streams of Dent blood were united, both having derived from one common ancestor. Along with other important personages of the day, General John Dent, his wife, Mrs. Sarah (Marshall) Dent, and their daughter, Mrs. Anne Herbert (Dent) Wilkinson — Jane's mother — sat for portraits by the noted painter of the Revolutionary era — Charles Willson Peale.

The world into which Jane Long was born was an exciting world of action in which the United States of America emerged from a comparatively young republic to full stature as a nation. In 1798 the United States was but twenty-two years old with her manifest destiny to the West as yet unfulfilled. It was the year that marked the beginning of a limited and undeclared war with France over the so-called "X. Y. Z. Affair," in which France demanded a loan and a bribe for French officials before dealing with American representatives. It was likewise the year that Congress set up a Department of the Navy to supplement the privateers and armed ships on the high seas and to protect American shipping against the Barbary pirates in the Mediterranean. In reactivating the Navy, which had not operated since 1783, the United States completed the building of the frigates the *United States*, the *Constitution*, and the *Constellation*. The year 1798 was the date of the passage of the Alien and Sedition Acts, which curtailed the rights of foreigners and permitted the president of the nation to deport undesirable aliens and those inimical to the welfare of the country.

The family's removal to Mississippi in 1811 had its effect on Jane Wilkinson's girlhood. In that year Mrs. Wilkinson moved her family from Maryland to Washington in the Mississippi Territory. Undoubtedly the fact that the famous relative General James Wilkinson lived in the South at the time was a factor in Mrs. Wilkinson's choice of the location. Certainly the family maintained close contact with General Wilkinson, who was Jane's guardian. Only a year later at the beginning of the War of 1812, Mrs. Wilkinson died. Orphaned at fourteen, Jane went to live with the family of her older sister, Mrs. Barbara Calvit, who resided at Propinquity, one of the most luxurious of the many ante-bellum plantations for which Natchez was famous. Twice orphaned, Jane had begun to develop a maturity that belied her youth. It was at this time that she also began to develop a vivacious and adventuresome spirit. Since some of Jane's characteristics possibly identified her with her guardian or possibly because he had sired only sons, General Wilkinson indulged his ward. Never having known her own male parent, Jane accepted her guardian as a father substitute and addressed him as "Uncle James." Meanwhile General Wilkinson spoiled his ward as if she had been the only child of a doting father. Jane was aware of General Wilkinson's prestige and, not unlike others, had found him charming.

A singularly handsome man and one of the most controversial names in American history, General Wilkinson was a man of divided loyalties who was best known for the Neutral Ground agreement and the exposure of Aaron Burr's conspiracy. Still few men of the time exceeded his national prominence. Royal Ornan Shreve in *The Finished Scoundrel* (Indianapolis, 1933, 14-15) states:

> He was a brigadier before his twenty-first birthday . . . He was an officer in the army for thirty-odd years, its commander in chief, under four presidents, for seventeen. His . . . trail covers the United States east of the Mississippi and more; it extended from Havana to Detroit, from Montreal to the City of Mexico. He laid out the town of Frankfort, Kentucky; built a mansion on Wilkinson Street later used as a state-house. In Wilkinson County, Mississippi, . . . he built Fort Adams, for a few years far southwestern corner of the United States . . . .

Although Wilkinson had earned his license to practice medicine at seventeen, he declined to enter the profession, preferring the military instead. On November 12, 1778, he was united in marriage with Anne Biddle of the socially elite Biddle family of Pennsylvania. Wilkinson's wife was a cousin to Captain James Biddle of the United States navy and his wealthy brother Nicholas Biddle, who later became president of the second bank of the

United States.

Known officially as "Number Thirteen" in the Spanish secret service, Wilkinson was the recipient of substantial remuneration for his espionage until 1800. His success in the service of Spain is a part of Spanish and American history.

The acquisition of the Louisiana Territory by the United States in 1803 had a direct bearing upon General Wilkinson. He was summoned to share with Governor C. C. Claiborne the honor of taking possession of the Louisiana Purchase. Only two years later, in 1805, Wilkinson was elevated to the governorship of that portion of the purchase above the thirty-third parallel with headquarters at St. Louis.

The Louisiana Purchase increased Spain's anxiety over her Texas eastern border. She considered the transaction by France a breach of faith and to discourage further American interest strengthened her fortifications in Texas. The United States retaliated in kind by placing troops under General Wilkinson's command along the eastern boundary. Such cities as New Orleans, Alexandria, Natchez, Natchitoches, and other settlements along the lower Mississippi and Red rivers soon became the asylum for renegades and lawbreakers generally. What was more, many Americans claimed Texas as a part of Louisiana.

Wilkinson allegedly took advantage of the precarious situation that ensued between the United States and Spain over the boundary dispute. He and Aaron Burr were said to have designed an elaborate plan to invade Mexico in 1806 for the purpose of exploiting the situation and establishing their own empire. They had expected to incite rebellion of the western states and add that territory to the kingdom with New Orleans as its capital.

But Burr talked too much and Wilkinson had to do an about face. Instead of going through with the plans, he betrayed Burr to President Jefferson. When Wilkinson saw Burr's army approaching from Blennerhasset's Island on the Ohio side of the river, he sent a special courier to the President that "treason was afloat" and assault upon the city of New Orleans imminent.

That same day, November 6, 1806, Wilkinson, as representative of the United States, concurred with Lieutenant Colonel Simon Herrera, acting for Spain, that the area between the Arroyo Hondo, on the east, and the Sabine River, on the west, should be considered as Neutral Ground until the two nations could negotiate a permanent treaty. It was generally thought that the Gulf of Mexico marked the southern boundary and the thirty-second parallel of latitude the northern perimeter.

It is of interest to note that, even though General Wilkinson's reputation suffered as a result of the Burr incident, he was finally exonerated in 1815. Another thing, Wilkinson had his loyal following among the leaders of the day, not the least of whom was President Jefferson himself.

Just as the family's move to Mississippi had left its impact on Jane's girlhood, so did the War of 1812 help to mold her future and start her on the road to destiny. At the termination of the war with the Battle of New Orleans January 8, 1815, the leisurely-paced, somnolent town of Natchez changed its image. As the year ending the war indicated a turning point in the relations of the United States with other nations, Natchez mushroomed into a center of feverish activity. Nátchez-Under-the-Hill, as the town was called, began its feast years in 1815, when fortunes were made overnight, pretentious Southern mansions set the standard for luxurious living, and men from all over the world descended upon it in search of adventure, fame, and riches. To American people in general the War of 1812 had established commercial independence, as the Revolutionary War had made political sovereignty possible. It was in this exhilarating atmosphere, much of which orbited around her distinguished kinsman and guardian, that Jane Wilkinson developed into young womanhood.

The manner in which Jane met and married Dr. James Long is like a scene from one of Sir Walter Scott's novels except for the transposition of time and place. Present is the conflict between the old order of tradition (the established world of the Wilkinsons) and the rising new culture (the uncertain new world Dr. Long proposed to create). The scene is even replete with its "castle" — the fabled Propinquity mansion, where also existed the institution of slavery — a system of vassalage much like that of the feudalism of mediaeval Europe.

Following the Battle of New Orleans, Dr. Long's company was based at Natchez and wounded soldiers were nursed in private homes of the town. Like other families, the inhabitants of Propinquity Plantation gave refuge to a sick soldier, who occupied one of the second story bedrooms. The soldier's attending physician was the officer with whom he had served — Dr. James Long.

A lieutenant in Carroll's Brigade, Dr. Long had been personally cited for spectacular bravery by his commander, General Andrew Jackson. A native of Virginia, Long had grown up in Tennessee. At the callow age of 15 an unsuccessful business venture had led him to the study of medicine. For two years he worked in his father's store in Tennessee and saved up six hundred dollars which he invested in a medical apprenticeship. Soon after obtaining his license to practice, he had joined the United States army.

Like other young ladies of her social class, young sixteen-year-old Jane attended a private academy or so-called "finishing school." When the doctor arrived to see his patient Jane was dressed to leave the residence for the academy which was close by. The school bell had just rung. Still Jane was in no haste to respond to its summons. Legend has it that the lovely little

Southern belle, who lived in one of the finest old mansions of the area was shamelessly admiring her own image in her mirror. Indeed her dark ringletted hair, mischievous brown eyes, and cream-white complexion — not to mention the green silk bonnet (one of her "Uncle James'" most recent extravagances) she was proudly adjusting were far more important to her than grammar recitations, spelling drills, and doing sums on her slate. Frankly, academy routine bored the young lady whose social poise was advanced for her age. At sixteen she was already a woman. Fortunately before her mother had passed away, she had painstakingly tutored her youngest daughter in the fundamentals accepted as suitable for young ladies of Jane's class: reading and writing, along with carding, spinning, weaving, embroidering, and quilting.

As Jane was about to pick up her book satchel and proceed to school with lagging feet, she heard the voice of her little Negro maid Kian. The black girl, who was only a few years younger and a close companion, had watched the doctor ascend the stairs. The romantically inclined Kian suggested that her mistress remain at home and meet the young doctor. In her enthusiasm she declared him to be the handsomest man in the world. Since Jane had not been attracted to the many suitors among her contemporaries in Natchez, the suggestion made sense. Accordingly, she discarded books and bonnet and awaited the doctor's return from the sick room. Hearing his footsteps on the stairs, she invited Dr. Long to engage in a game of backgammon. He eagerly consented. The tall Virginian's impressive physique and martial air impressed Jane instantly.

Soon the two young people (Long was scarcely five years older than Jane) were more absorbed in each other than in the game they were playing. It was said that the doctor made a point of losing so that he would have an excuse for returning — to present Jane with the forfeit — a pair of gloves.

The next day as the handsome doctor assisted the lady in pulling on the gloves, he cleverly remarked that he wished "the hand that gave might go with the gift." The compliment was not wasted.

Dr. Long's visit to Propinquity became increasingly more frequent, and everyone concerned became aware that the couple were getting serious. In accordance with accepted nineteenth century etiquette, Long paid a formal visit to General Wilkinson and requested permission to marry his ward. For a number of reasons Jane's guardian disapproved of the match. In the first place, he thought Jane was too young. In the second, the Wilkinsons had learned that Dr. Long was an unpredictable man with irreconcilable extremes in his temperament that made him appear to be unstable.

Jane pouted at her guardian's decision, even became defiant. Mrs. Wilkinson, whom Jane called "Aunt Anne," even tried to convince her that marriage to a professional soldier and glory seeker had its disadvantages. Mrs.

Wilkinson knew by lonely experience whereof she spoke. As involved as her husband was in army administration and his many other affairs, he had been obliged to neglect his own family. Jane, on the other hand, felt that she could persuade James to resign his commission and settle down.

The Wilkinsons remained adamant in their stand against the marriage. Equally inflexible in her determination to go ahead with the nuptials, Jane sought a way to disregard her relatives' opposition. It was not long before the couple put their wits together and arrived at a solution to the problem. The law in the Mississippi Territory held that an orphan, upon attaining a certain age, could select her own guardian. It was as simple as that: Long having achieved his majority, Jane chose him as a replacement for General Wilkinson. Finally the family relented somewhat and the wedding was solemnized at Propinquity on May 14, 1815. It is not a matter of record that General Jame Wilkinson attended the ceremony or gave the bride away.

After a two-months' wedding trip, the couple located at Port Gibson, where Dr. Long began to practice medicine half-heartedly. Restless and preoccupied with the accumulation of wealth, the couple moved to a lavish plantation at Walnut Hills. Here their first child, Ann Herbert, was born November 26, 1816. Still restless, the Longs sold the property and moved back to Natchez. In three years Dr. Long had tried three different vocations with indifferent success. The last of these was a business partnership with W. E. Walker of Natchez, which had become the gateway to the frontier.

Meanwhile the Neutral Ground continued to seethe with adventurers and unsavory characters seeking refuge and escape from prosecution. Simultaneously Mexico was making strides in her long struggle for independence from Spain. Into this unsettled state of affairs was released the bombshell of the Adams-Onis (or Florida) Treaty on February 22, 1819. The treaty agreed upon by President John Quincy Adams and Don Luis de Onis, Spanish minister, finally settled the boundary dispute over which the Neutral Ground had been created. The most objectionable provision was that the United States relinquished its claim to Texas in exchange for Spain's recognition of America's rights to Florida. In the opinions of many the action amounted to the trading of Texas for Florida, which the nation already virtually possessed. Furthermore, the belief that Texas belonged to the United States as a part of the Louisiana Purchase was widespread. Even the two men — Robert R. Livingston and James Monroe — who handled the $15,000,000 transaction, held this view. Later Thomas Jefferson felt that the United States had a valid claim to Texas.

With Mexico winning the conflict with Spain, it looked as if Texas would eventually belong to that nation. Opposition to the treaty spread quickly over the United States. However, since the territories of Louisiana and Mississippi were vitally affected, the movement against it centered in

Natchez. Consequently a mass meeting was convened in Natchez in May of 1819, to organize an invasion to liberate Texas. Naturally among the men who enthusiastically supported the expedition were the dissenters occupying the Neutral Ground and other border characters in quest of adventure. Still there were other ardent supporters such as General Wilkinson, General John Adair, and Dr. Long. In the shortest time the sum of $500,000 was raised to finance the expedition. General Wilkinson was a heavy subscriber, and it was said that Dr. Long invested his entire personal fortune in the venture. As an inducement to recruiting, every soldier was promised a league of Texas land. Despite the fact that the Wilkinsons had disapproved of Dr. Long in the beginning, the two families had maintained close contact. Long had personally met Phillip Nolan, General Wilkinson's secretary and agent, who had brought back glowing accounts of the potentialities of Texas from his forays into the area to round up wild horses. He was likewise impressed with the grandiose schemes and visions of Wilkinson himself. Accordingly, when General John Adair declined to head the enterprise and the choice fell to Long, he eagerly accepted it. This was the vocation for which the 26-year-old visionary and volatile Dr. Long apparently considered himself most suited.

Since she was expecting her second child, Dr. Long insisted that Jane remain behind and possibly join him later. Barely escaping arrest, the filibuster, now elevated to the rank of general, left Natchez June 17, 1819, with seventy-five men. By the time the contingent had reached its destination of Nacogdoches on June 22, recruits en route had swelled the number to 300.

Taking up quarters in the Old Stone Fort, Long proclaimed the independence of Texas on June 23, 1819, and began the disposition of the public lands. Long's declaration of independence was publicized in the October 18 edition of the *London Courier*. Immediately Long organized a provisional government with the cooperation of his forces and the citizens of Nacogdoches. The combined group named the leader president of the republic and commander in chief of the armed forces.

Even though Spanish authority in Texas at the time was weak, Long underestimated it. He scattered his forces from the Red River to Galveston Bay, thus making himself and his men vulnerable to attack. His situation was doubly precarious inasmuch as the American officers at Fort Jessup prevented quantities of provisions from reaching him. To offset this condition, he opened trade with the Indians. The situation soon developed into an emergency and Long was faced with the problem of obtaining aid elsewhere.

It was at this strategic time that Jane finally arrived at Nacogdoches. She had waited until after the birth of another daughter, whom she named Rebecca, and had left the children with the Calvits, who had moved to

Alexandria, Louisiana. Mrs. Long made the trip against the advice of her doctor and the wishes of her family. After having begun her journey by boat, she had taken a carriage from Louisiana. It had been an arduous journey fraught with many hardships. Forced to abandon the carriage, Jane Long, accompanied by her maid Kian and a cavalcade of men headed by Randal Jones (whom Long had sent to escort her safely), rode into Texas upon the back of a mule. From the very beginning Mrs. Long had considered herself her husband's collaborator in the expedition and would let nothing deter her.

Long established his wife at the Old Stone Fort, but her happiness at being reunited with him was shortlived. As part of his strategy to replenish supplies, Long had hoped for aid from another veteran of the Battle of New Orleans — the pirate Jean Lafitte based on Galveston Island. His previous attempts having been unsuccessful, Long deemed it expedient to make the trip to secure aid himself. Almost immediately after Jane had rejoined him, he left the base at Nacogdoches in charge of Captain Hamlin Cook and set out with a detail of thirteen men bound for Galveston. What Long did not know, or could not take into account, was that Jean and his brother Pierre also engaged in espionage for Spain when it suited their plans.

The fact was that Governor Antonio Martinez had known of Long's occupation of Nacogdoches as early as June 17, 1819, and immediately issued orders to prepare the Interior Provinces for defense. Accordingly General Arredondo was ordered to reconnoiter the Sabine with a cavalry force of 500 men and to recruit twice that number if the situation warranted. In September Colonel Ignacio Perez was assigned a command at San Antonio. He left his base on September 27 with a force of 550 men. The advance was delayed by the Indians setting fire to the plains. Still the Indians also played into the hands of the Spanish by informing them of the eight Anglo-Americans trading with them. Spanish spies had also obtained the intelligence that the fort at Nacogdoches was practically without defense. As a result of this information, Perez decided on a number of raids to intercept the enemy. Long and his men did not learn of the approach of the Spanish until they reached the Coushatta Village on the Trinity. Although he tried to get word to the outposts for the men to concentrate at Nacogdoches, it was too late. They had already been wiped out. What was also discouraging, Long's confidence in Captain Cook was misplaced, and the garrison had become demoralized. Long hastened back to Nacogdoches arriving only two days in advance of the invading forces. He had sent word to Jane to await him at the house of a friend. But she had exercised better judgment and had crossed the Sabine into the safety of United States territory. Long had gotten word to the remaining forces at the Coushatta camp to retreat to Bolivar Point, a peninsula on Galveston Bay, to await his arrival. Long himself followed the other evacuees across the Sabine on October 26. Upon crossing into the United States, the Longs received the news of the death of the baby Rebecca. Long sent Jane back to her sister's home in Alexandria and rejoined the remnant of his men at Bolivar Point. Through the assistance of the Indians on the Trinity, Randal and James Jones had escaped into Louisiana. Thus in less than three months had ended the first abortive expedition of General James Long to free Texas from the yoke of Spain.

After speedily reorganizing his men at Bolivar Point, Long plunged into a fund raising campaign to finance his second expedition. He carried his campaign first to New Orleans and Natchitoches without success. At Alexandria, where he rejoined Jane and her family, and at Natchez his efforts to raise capital met with encouraging response. He was so favorably impressed with the reaction at Natchez that he prevailed upon Jane to return with him to Bolivar Point and consider establishing a permanent home somewhere in Texas. About this time the couple encountered Warren D. C. Hall, a friend of Lafitte and a veteran of the Gutierrez-Magee expedition, and persuaded him to join them. With his newly acquired funds, Long purchased a sloop for the return trip and stocked it with provisions.

The three persons cast anchor at Bolivar Point April 6, 1820. They found the weather mild, flowers blooming luxuriantly, a profusion of wild game, and the bayous brimful of fish and oysters. In his absence Long's men had fared well. They had been able to exchange venison and other wild game for powder from the pirate Lafitte. The future looked most promising.

Soon after their arrival Lafitte sent over an invitation for the three to dine with him. Hall and Jane accepted but Long declined the honor of dining with the pirate no doubt because he suspected that Lafitte had betrayed him to the Spanish. Lafitte was about to abandon his island stronhold forever. He had been ordered to evacuate Galveston by an officer of the United States Navy and the moratorium extended him had expired. Still he delayed weighing anchor until the beautiful Jane Long could come aboard his ship the *Pride* fcr a sumptuous dinner. Years later Mrs. Long remembered the occasion with pleasure. Judging by later accounts, she was the only lady present at the elegant board. Indeed the experience of being toasted by adventurous men who raised golden goblets of the rarest vintage wine in the world to her was a far cry from the lady's entry into Texas astride a mule — but likewise the center of attention escorted by an admiring cavalcade.

Soon Long found it necessary to raise more capital for the enterprise. He left the fort in command of W. W. Walker and he, together with Jane and Hall, returned to Louisiana. The Longs retrieved their daughter, Ann, at Alexandria and proceeded to New Orleans. In the crescent city Long finally interested two American capitalists and the firm of Brant and Foster in the enterprise. The capitalists agreed to underwrite the second expedition to free

Texas upon the conditions that they determine policy, have a voice in the making of major decisions, and that the recently released political prisoner from Havana, General Jose Felix Trespalacios head the operation. Their position was that a Mexican in command would be more acceptable to the insurgents of Mexico than an American. Ben Milam, John Austin, and the Mexican's nephew were with the general. Long did not like the terms but really had no choice. Moreover, the backing was generous. It had required six weeks to accomplish the transaction, and during the time Jane had made the most of the reunion with her husband and daughter.

Once again Long left his wife behind while he impatiently hastened on ahead. Before departing, he had arranged for Jane to travel on a new ship, the *Three Sisters*, under the protection of Milam and Austin. Mrs. Long, remembering the loss of the baby Rebecca, eventually decided to remain with little Ann, who was not well. Despite the delay, Milam and Austin reached Bolivar Point at the same time that Long did, on June 1, 1820.

Although Long was eager to attack La Bahia, as Goliad was called, he was persuaded by the Expedition's sponsors to wait until sufficient Anglo-Americans could settle Texas to insure him of success. Prohibited from fighting, Long initiated a heavy program of work. He improved the fort, established a government, drew up laws, and declared Galveston, which he renamed *Las Casas*, a port of entry for the (nonexistent) Republic of Texas on August 30.

In spite of the fact that he needed men badly, Long was impatient to move against San Antonio. Again one of his backers prevented him. This time the sponsor reminded him that he should wait until General Trespalacios, who was the actual, at least titular, head of the operation, could join him. As an alternative, Long led his dissatisfied soldiers into a battle against the Karankawa Indians. In a surprise attack, as the Indians were engaged in a night of wild orgies and drunken revelry aboard a boat they had taken, Long and his men killed thirty-three warriors and captured two Indian boys.

Even with a warrant out for his arrest for transporting contraband articles of war, Long slipped back to Calcasieu, Louisiana, where Jane was living temporarily. With the improved conditions at the fort, Long felt that Jane could very well return with the little daughter and Kian. Other women had now joined their husbands at the garrison, two of whom, the wives of Doctors Allen and Edwards, would make suitable companions for Mrs. Long. True enough, Mrs. Long's first impression of the Point had been favorable.

Immediately Mrs. Long began to make preparations. By the following December (1820), she arrived at Bolivar Point with her devoted little maid Kian and daughter, Ann. She had brought such personal items as were possible to add to the family's comfort. She did her best to convert their living quarters into what approximated a crude home of sorts. For a time her happiness exceeded all bounds. She had her baby with her, the companionship of her maid and loyal friend, and was again reunited with her husband. Besides she was a Wilkinson through whose veins coursed the spirit and courage that transforms virgin wastelands into centers of civilization — and she wanted to do her part.

The next month (November) General Trespalacios arrived at the garrison to take charge. In the interest of his employers, he insisted that the men work. As if that were not enough to insure his unpopularity, he paid the soldiers with treasury notes which New Orleans merchants refused to honor. As a result several men deserted. When Trespalacios went to New Orleans to seek further aid, some of the discontented soldiers followed him and made an attempt on his life. He was forced to go into hiding until Long could come to his rescue. In late August both Long and Trespalacios returned with a few new recruits and a sloop laden with fresh supplies.

At the same time that the two leaders of the expedition were in New Orleans, Moses Austin was in San Antonio conferring with Governor Martinez on his proposed plans for the colonization of Texas. Austin informed the governor of Long's almost destitute situation at Bolivar Point. Governor Martinez had been aware of Long's activities and assured the colonizer that he was prepared to eliminate Long at the opportune time.

Soon after the two leaders' return to the fort in August, news reached the garrison of Agustin de Iturbide's Plan of Iguala, which meant that Mexico was grinding down the revolution and the pretexts for filibustering no longer existed. Since this development affected Long's plans directly, the government of the operation voted to send two men to Mexico to determine how the new government felt about Long's enterprise. Accordingly, Trespalacios and Milam left on this mission August 20, 1821.

Almost immediately after the men sailed, reports reached the fort that La Bahia and San Antonio had declared for independence. As a matter of fact, none of the colonists had been particularly loyal to Spain and the two towns were virtually independent already. However, this latter news convinced Long that, if he wished to have a part in the liberation of Texas, he could delay no longer. Therefore on September 19, 1821, he left prematurely with a fleet of three vessels and fifty-two men for Copano Bay. Before leaving, he exacted a pledge from Jane not to leave the Point until his return. He estimated his absence would not exceed three weeks. With luck he might be able to return before the birth of the third child Jane was expecting in December.

For the first few days following Long's departure, life at the Point was pleasant enough. The small close-knit group of women and children, together with the soldiers — possibly no more than twenty-five — left to man the fort, spent the time leisurely enjoying the scenery, fishing the Gulf, and scanning the horizon for sails. But when Long's alloted three weeks had expired without any news whatsoever, the inhabitants of the garrison became apprehensive. When the weeks lengthened to a month, then six weeks, there followed a steady withdrawal. As they left, the families and the soldiers took the necessary equipment and supplies to insure survival. Each group evacuating the fort tried to prevail upon Mrs. Long to accompany them. They promised to see her and the two children safely to any destination she chose. They pointed out to Mrs. Long the dangers of remaining. Aside from the problems of obtaining food and supplies, there was no doctor to deliver the baby she was expecting in December. Again there were across the bay the hostile Indians, who had taken possession of the island since Lafitte's abandonment of it. Against the cannibalistic Karankawas she would have no defense. Even if the Indians had not posed a threat, Jane's occupation of the Point could subject her to possible attack from the Mexicans. Mrs. Long declined all proffers of help. Repeatedly she told her friends that she felt it her duty to await at the fort for her husband's return. Not once did her faith in his return waver.

Thus Mrs. Long made her choice. Finally the sole inhabitants at Bolivar Point were the twenty-three-year-old woman, six-year-old Ann, twelve-year-old Kian, and a mongrel called "Galveston." The evacuees had exhausted the food supply and left only a small quantity of ammunition, a few surplus muskets, a single cannon, some fishhooks, and a single fishing line. The three persons ate the birds Jane shot and the fish she caught. Day after day, Mrs. Long, still hoping for her husband's return, walked the beach searching for the sails that never appeared. As if to underscore her loneliness, the shell of Lafitte's gutted Red House and three stark trees stood like ghost sentinels of the past. The only sound besides the booming surf was the occasional and almost intolerable cries of seagulls and pelicans.

December brought in one of the most inclement snow storms in the history of Galveston. The blizzard froze the bay between the island and the peninsula completely. The fort being for the most part roofless, Mrs. Long and the two children were obliged to take shelter in an improvised tent. On the night of December 21, 1821, the fierce north wind mingled with the cries of a newborn baby girl. Snow fell so heavily that it ripped through the tent and covered the bed where mother and baby lay. Not only was there no attending physician present, there was no help at all. Besides the young mother had the additional responsibility of nursing Kian, who was delirious with a fever. Although the claim has been questioned, some historians insist that the infant was the first child of Anglo-American descent to be born in Texas. With Christmas only a few days away, Mrs. Long named the baby Mary James to honor her missing husband and in memory of another mother who gave birth to her child in a manger in Bethlehem centuries before.

The morning following the birth of her third child, Mrs. Long and little Ann gathered frozen fish and preserved them in the brine of an empty pickle barrel. Christmas Day came uneventfully at Bolivar Point. Just as she had done on other days, Ann searched for moccasin prints around the fort. Kian had taught the child the game with more serious motive than she had explained.

The day after Christmas Captain Rafael Gonzales and a detail of six men from Monterrey brought Mrs. Long a message from her husband. The letter, which no doubt had been smuggled out with considerable difficulty, stated tersely that Long was a prisoner in Mexico but was well. The men had possibly brought food. They remained at the fort two days undoubtedly for the purpose of trying to convince Mrs. Long that she should let them escort her to safety on the mainland. But having learned that her husband was alive, Mrs. Long was more determined to wait for him as she had promised.

A few days later when Kian's fever had subsided, she and Mrs. Long seined the bayou for mullet to use for bait to fish the Gulf. Mrs. Long baited her single line a day afterwards and prayed for a strike. For some reason she had tied the line around her waist and when the strike came she was almost drawn into the Gulf. She hastily untied the line and it slipped through her fingers as an enormous redfish swam away with it. The incident was doubly discouraging. The severity of winter had decreased the quantity of birds. Now the little family would have to subsist solely upon a diet of oysters from the bay.

But how to provide food for the children and herself was not Mrs. Long's most pressing problem. She thought constantly of the menace of the Indians across the bay. It was only wishful thinking, but she hoped that they were not aware of her true plight. She felt that they would not dare attack if they thought the fort was still manned. What would she do if they decided to attack? Then suddenly one morning when the wintry blast was at its peak, Jane Long answered her own question.

Kian saw the canoe flotilla of the Karankawas rowing for the Point and rent the icy air with a scream. Quickly Mrs. Long confirmed the slave girl's report. Canoes bearing the hideous warriors fantastically painted for warfare were heading straight for the garrison. Since it had been too heavy to carry away, the evacuating soldiers had left a single cannon. Losing no time, Mrs. Long shouted to Kian to point the cannon in the direction of the approaching attackers. As Kian obeyed, Mrs. Long realized that no standard flew from the fort's flagpole. To add to the pretext that the fort was manned, there had to be one. In an instant she hoisted the first thing she saw — a discarded red-flannel petticoat. Then she applied the tinder and exploded the cannon with a dexterity surprising to herself, its loud detonation echoing across the bay. She had not hit her target but her ruse had apparently worked. After a moment's hesitation, the seven-feet-tall oarsmen reversed themselves and headed back to the island. Evidently the Indians remember the lesson General Long had taught them: not to risk attacking the white man in his stronghold.

With her red "flag" waving defiantly, Mrs. Long detonated the cannon at regular intervals to strengthen the deception that soldiers occupied the fort. In support of her mistress, Kian resorted to wearing an abandoned soldier's uniform when she went to the bay for oysters. While the campfires still burned nightly on Galveston Island, the Karankawas, evidently convinced that the fortress was manned, maintained a healthy respect for Fort Bolivar.

Thus the old year ended and 1822 made its appearance. Another month passed and for three days the inhabitants of the Point went without food. Kian was gathering driftwood on the beach when she saw three men approaching. She quickly relayed the news to Jane. Mrs. Long rushed out to meet the visitors. But, upon seeing her, they ran away. It could have been that her appearance had frightened them. Or they might have mistaken Mrs. Long for an Indian woman, which would indicate that the hostile tribe had taken over the fort. Indeed after all she had experienced, the once lovely Southern belle must have borne little resemblance to her former image.

Hungry and depressed, Mrs. Long walked painfully back along the beach to return to the fort, her head lowered in despair. She had taken only a few halting steps when she discovered what looked like a string caught in the sand. Aimlessly she reached down and disentangled it. Amazingly, as she continued to pull, she discovered that it was the fishing line that the large redfish had jerked away some four weeks ago. What was more, incredible as it may seem, there was the fish — still edible — on the end of the line. Mrs. Long, who was devotedly religious, considered the incident a miracle and a direct answer to her prayers for survival.

Kian continued to go to the beach each day as a lookout. Not long after she reported to her mistress the seeing of the three men, she noted sails appearing on the water. As quickly as possible, Mrs. Long went to the beach to signal. One of the three vessels responded. It was a sloop with fifteen male passengers aboard, the first of Stephen F. Austin's colonists. The men included the three who had been frightened earlier by Mrs. Long's appearance. They had heard about Long's imprisonment but had not known about her occupation of the fort during his absence. The vessels anchored in the bay that night and each shared their food with Mrs. Long and the children. The next day one of the ships proceeded on its course to Matamoros, one ran aground, and the third sailed toward the Brazos. The crew of the latter offered Mrs. Long passage to Austin's colony but she declined, still clinging to the hope that the next ship would restore her husband to her. Other vessels moored in the bay and, for the most part, brought conflicting news of Long and his men.

Fort Bolivar had been Mrs. Long's home for over a year, and for four months she had kept it alone except for the children. Still her resolve to remain was diminishing. Finally when old friends of earlier years insisted that she accompany them to Austin's colony, she accepted. Certainly on that morning in March of 1822 Mrs. Long took her departure with mixed feelings. She had known happiness at the fort with her husband and family. And though Bolivar Point had been a promising symbol in the beginning, she had also experienced an ordeal there that exceeded the wildest imaginings and defied human understanding.

Mrs. Long settled down in Austin's colony on the Brazos and began to make a new life for herself and her household. At San Felipe she renewed acquaintance with two old friends, Randal and James Jones, who had been members of Long's first abortive expedition.

After moving to San Felipe Mrs. Long learned of her husband's death in Mexico City. Abil Terrill, a trader along the coast, had promised her that he would find out what had happened to Long when he reached Matamoros and write her the details. Terrill's letter dispatched from Refugio, presents the Mexican version of Long's death, which was said to have been accidental. Designed to convey solace to the widow and to give as favorable an account of the incident as was possible under the circumstances, the letter was preserved by Mrs. Long. Whether she accepted the version or not, the letter did give her some hope of obtaining a settlement from the Mexican government. A transcript of the document follows as it appears in *Lamar Papers*, II, 120-121:

> Painful as it may be to your feelings, I conceive it my duty to give you a plain and strait account of the untimely death of Genl. Long. — He had been but ten days in Mexico City when the circumstance took place.
>
> Genl. Long was well recd. in Mexico City, & had recd. several visits together with many invitations from our English Col., one of which he was about to return, when he was hailed by a Centinel and ordered to stop, at the same time, Genl. Long put his hand to his side pocket, to draw a paper. (His Passport) The Centinel supposing it to be for the purpose of drawing his side fire arms to defend himself, at which time the Centinel fired at Genl. Long; and the ball entered his side & passed thro' him; he expired in a few minutes.
>
> His death was much regretted by the inhabitants in general. The Congress have it in contemplation, as soon as they get through the hurry of business as respects the Govt., to make a hansome appropriation for you & children & support.
>
> Mr. Sulivan gives the above statements in the presence of those whom accompanied him and was at the interment, which was attended

with a great concourse of people, exclusive of 40 coaches and that every respect was paid. He was not buried with the honors of war in consequence of his not being a Catholic —

Genl. Lopas [Lopez] is Commandant of Monterrey. Col Trespalascios is Governor of Texas and Col. of the militia left Mexico some time ago for St Antonio, is supposed to be at that place at this time. 500 troups are to be stationed at said place, about 40 troops leave this place for Labardee in 3 days.

Signed
Abil Terrill

Other accounts of Long's death indicate that he was assassinated as a result of political intrigue. Nonetheless, all accounts concur on three major points: the date, April 8, 1822; the place, Mexico City; and the gun that killed Long was in the hands of a sentinel.

The general consensus of descendants was that after Long's release from prison in Monterrey (instigated by the American minister Joel R. Poinsett), he went under guard to Mexico City. His object was to get a treaty ratified and to secure the promised indemnity for his investment of $80,000 in the two unsuccessful expeditions. Upon, arrival, he had purportedly turned his papers over to the proper officials who scheduled a day for him to return for them.

On the appointed day Long entered the courtyard of the Old Inquisition building. When he reached in his breastpocket for his passport he was felled with the document in his hand. The sentinel alleged that he thought Long was in the process of drawing a pistol. There was no reason for Long to draw a pistol. There was valid reason why he should not. Some descendants believe that the treaty named Long the provisional governor of Texas under the government of Mexico. This claim is highly conjectural as Long's subsequent arrest and imprisonment first in San Antonio, then later in Mexico, is totally incompatible with such an appointment.

Ben Milam, John Austin, and other friends of Long were of the opinion that Trespalacios, jealous of Long's political influence in Texas, paid the assassin to kill him. Another possibility was that both Trespalacios and the head of the government, Augustin de Iturbide, collaborated to eliminate Long, as both stood to gain with the filibusterer out of the way. Assuredly the new government, which had ignored Long's efforts and imprisoned him for his pains, had no intention of honoring his claim of a debt of $80,000. Like the man from Mancha, Long was tilting with windmills.

At any rate, Long was dead and his body consigned to an unmarked grave in the Mexican capital, Iturbide was the emperor on the throne, and Trespalacios was the Mexican governor-general of Texas presiding at San Antonio. Regardless of what Mrs. Long believed concerning the way in which Long met his death, the final confirmation of his demise spelled the end of a chapter. If her gallant husband had attempted to create his own empire at twenty-six and had died as a result at twenty-nine, Mrs. Long still faced the responsibility of supporting herself and their children and liquidating Long's debts.

Consequently on September 9, 1822, she began a journey to San Antonio to try to obtain money from the government. Since Trespalacios had sent her a personal invitation she was optimistic. To make the trip she engaged the services of Randal and James Jones as escorts. A total of nine persons comprised the group of travelers, including three Negro men brought along to help with the chores. Mrs. Long had insisted upon taking her two children and Kian along. She herself carried the infant Mary James in her arms. For the party of nine there were only four mounts; hence some were obliged to walk. Little Ann rode a pack mule.

The motley little cavalcade were five weeks en route, arriving at San Antonio October 17, 1823. Although Trespalacios played well the part of the courteous host, he had no money to advance to Mrs. Long. After giving her horse to the Joneses for the return trip to San Felipe, Mrs. Long and her entourage took an apartment in San Antonio. It had been necessary for her to pawn or sell her valuables to take care of expenses along the way and to finance herself at the capital. Mrs. Long and her group had hardly moved into their lodgings before Iturbide was overthrown and forced to abdicate March 19, 1823. As a result of this political upheaval, Trespalacios also abdicated and made hasty plans to return to Mexico. No doubt to save face, he extended Mrs. Long an invitation to accompany him and his wife. Since Trespalacios had neither money nor political prestige, Mrs. Long declined the invitation. Before leaving San Antonio, the former governor did restore to Mrs. Long the arms and ammunition confiscated when Long and his men had been imprisoned in San Antonio in the fall of 1821. She converted the firearms into cash with which she purchased a horse and a mule.

About this time an affluent friend of former years arrived at San Antonio with a pack train bound for Monterrey. He contacted Mrs. Long, provided food for her, and advanced her a loan of $2,000. He offered Mrs. Long and her household safe escort to the United States upon his return. Jane had expressed a desire to visit her sisters in Louisiana and Mississippi. Mrs. Long's visit to San Antonio extended to ten months. In that time the young widow had undergone a complete regeneration. She had become a different person — a woman restored in health and revived in spirit. Above everything else, she was once again a beautiful woman imbued with a zest for living.

The wealthy friend with the pack train returned to San Antonio in September of 1823. On September 6, 1823, the travelers set out on their journey to the United States. They reached their destination of Alexandria, Louisiana, one month to a day after their departure. It had been three eventful and arduous years since Mrs. Long had seen her relatives.

She spent six months with the Calvits in Alexandria and equal time with another sister in Rodney, Mississippi. On the day of her departure from Rodney, she met Ben Milam, who had first tried to contact her at Natchez. Milam had been first imprisoned in Saltillo in 1821. He attributed his arrest and incarceration to the betrayal of Trespalacios. He was arrested again in Monterrey, taken to Saltillo as a prisoner, then transferred to prison in Mexico. As noted earlier, Milam held Trespalacios responsible for Long's assassination. Milam's second arrest was made after two of his confederates informed the authorities that Milam and others were plotting to kill Trespalacios. Through the intervention of Poinsett, he was released November 11, 1822. Milam had painstakingly preserved Long's papers, personal effects, and clothes, which he turned over to Mrs. Long.

While visiting in the home of the Millers in Rodney in 1824, Mrs. Long had the misfortune of losing the baby Mary James, for whose birth she had been called "The Mother of Texas." The reason for the baby's death is not recorded.

In December of 1825 Mrs. Long returned to San Felipe accompanied by the Calvits, whom she had persuaded to join her. Even though she did not prosper the three years she spent in the centerpiece of Austin's colony, Mrs. Long occupied a special place in it. She took an active part in community affairs and contributed much to the social life. Because of her frontier experience, Austin sought her counsel from time to time and valued her judgment. He tried to assist her in getting the subsidy from the Mexican government to which Terrill had referred. Also in 1827 he confirmed Mrs. Long's title to her headright league located in the vicinity of the old log fort identified as Fort Bend, which served as the nucleus later for the town of Richmond.

At the site Milam, who had returned to Texas and was colonizing Pecan Point, erected a comfortable cabin for her. Milam was Mrs. Long's benefactor in numerous ways. It was rumored in the colony that the two were sweethearts. Assuredly Mrs. Long could not have chosen a more handsome mate and a man with whom she had so much in common. Over six feet tall, Milam was a commanding figure whose dark eyes and black hair were attractive. There is the possibility that the two might have wed, had fate not removed Milam from the scene in his untimely death at the siege of Bexar on December 7, 1835.

In 1828, on her thirtieth birthday, Mrs. Long decided to relocate at Fort Bend. Despite her reverses at San Felipe, she retained a hopeful outlook. She still needed money badly to support her family and repay her debts which had continued to mount. In addition, there was the expense of Ann's future education to consider.

The year after moving to Fort Bend Mrs. Long sent fifteen-year-old Ann back to Natchez to attend school. In 1831 Mrs. Long returned to Louisiana for a visit and possibly to attend her daughter's wedding solemnized at Natchez that year. Ann was married to Edward Winston of Washington, Mississippi, in January of 1831. The following April the young couple came to Texas to make their home with Mrs. Long.

The four years at Fort Bend had not brought Mrs. Long the financial success for which she had hoped. For this reason, together with her expanded family and outstanding debts, she felt the necessity to move again. The majority of Austin's first colonists had settled in the two districts of Fort Bend and Brazoria. Daily the route between San Felipe and Brazoria was increasing in importance and was destined to become the most extensively traveled in Texas in 1835. As a result of these factors, Mrs. Long opened an inn at Brazoria in 1832.

Early Texas history literally revolved around Mrs. Long as the proprietor of two inns: the boarding house at Brazoria (prior to the Revolution) and another at Richmond (established during the first year of the Republic). From the year 1832 Mrs. Long's economy improved. And even better still, now that she was reconciled to her husband's death, she transferred her unstinted devotion to the cause of Texas. As an ardent supporter for the movement to separate Texas from Mexico, she influenced others. Also as the operator of two inns, Mrs. Long came in contact with all of the leading men of the day. Just as she had known intimately Stephen F. Austin, Ben Milam, the Jones brothers, and James Bowie, who came to Texas with Long's first expedition; so would she come to know and exert influence upon Erastus (Deaf) Smith, Anson Jones, David G. Burnet, "Three-Legged Willie" Williamson, William Barret Travis, Sam Houston, and Mirabeau B. Lamar. But it was the latter three with whom her ties were closest.

It is true that Mrs. Long held a fascination for men. However, her dedication to Texas and her work for the so-called war party, exceeded any emotional attachment. This was particularly true after the death of her close friend, Ben Milam. It was said that William Barret Travis was infatuated with Mrs. Long. Certainly references in his diary reveal an admiration for her as an older woman of character. The enterprising young attorney always stayed at her public house in Brazoria when legal business took him there. Occasionally he represented Mrs. Long in the collection of an over-due account. Again he collected from her for other clients, accepting room and board as part of the settlement. At other times when Travis' gambling losses, or his custom of lending almost anyone a few dollars, left him short, Mrs. Long would extend him credit. The devotion of both to the Texas cause for independence cemented a bond between them.

At the time Mrs. Long opened the tavern at Brazoria, two pertinent factors affected Austin's policy. First, the increasing population (over 10,000 at the time) had left its impact. Texas was no longer a place of defeat and confusion. It was rapidly evolving into a frontier settlement essentially American in character rather than Mexican. Second, the repeated efforts of the United States to purchase the province stimulated Mexican concern. As a result the Mexican government passed the odious Law of 1830 prohibiting further immigration into Texas from the United States. All of this added to Empresario Austin's burden. While he was still trying to maintain his cautious policy of moderation, the colonists were attempting to achieve union through a series of consultations. Antagonism to the Mexican government became so strong in 1833 that the colonists held a second convention in which they demanded statehood, separation from Coahuila, and repeal of the unjust Immigration Law of 1830. Austin took these grievances to Mexico to present personally.

Meanwhile, Mexico had undergone another political somersault. After representing the colonists, Austin was arrested, without being formally charged, and held prisoner in Mexico for twenty-eight months. While holding the Texas leader in prison, the Mexican government, headed by Santa Anna, sent Colonel Juan N. Almonte to obtain statistical data to use in the invasion of Texas and to gain time by delaying the start of the war. As Almonte described the purpose of the mission, it was to survey the needs of the colonists and present them to the Mexican government.

Nobody was fooled by Almonte's fabrications, least of all Mrs. Long. She entertained the Mexican officer in her boarding house and went ahead with preparation for the Revolution. Right under her guest's nose, Mrs. Long and other members of the war party stocked an arsenal in a brick outhouse on her property. The first powder to be used for the Revolution was stored at Mrs. Long's.

Austin's release was timed to coincide with the end of Almonte's visit for obvious reasons. Finally released in July of 1835, Austin arrived in Texas September 1. To mark the empresario's return, the citizens of Brazoria tendered him a banquet at Mrs. Long's tavern on September 8, 1835, at which he made the keynote address. More than a thousand Anglo-Americans listened to Austin enthusiastically for over an hour. No longer the conservative advising compromise, Austin urged unity of action among the colonists. His impassioned phrases were, in the opinion of many, tantamount to a declaration of war. Later the excited guest danced until dawn. Much of the planning for this gala and significant political event was under the personal supervision of Mrs. Long. Thus her tavern at Brazoria was the setting for the Republic's conception.

With Austin's return, the war party gained ascendancy. No longer were the Constitution of 1824 and statehood the objectives. Immediate separation of Texas from Mexico without legal technicalities was the goal — in short nothing less than independence. Into this climate moved Sam Houston, who had been in Texas since December of 1832. In conformity with his mission, Houston had immediately affiliated with the war party after settling down at Nacogdoches. It was inevitable that he and Jane Long would meet. Their common interest in Texas independence would have brought them together in any event. Like most prominent men of the time, the former governor of Tennessee boarded at Mrs. Long's hotel in Brazoria. Since it was the strategic location as the chief port of entry into Texas, many famous personages made ingress through Brazoria and partook of Mrs. Long's hospitality. Just when Houston first met Mrs. Long is not certain. The conjecture is that they met soon after Houston was appointed commander in chief of the Texas army for the first time. It is reasonable to think that he probably met Mrs. Long some time between his very first appointment as head of the Texas forces and his assumption of command at Gonzales on March 11, 1836. It is said that Mrs. Long gave Houston a powder horn that Lafitte had presented to her. She no doubt presented the curious object to Houston to wish him luck at the beginning of the campaign. Perhaps she received some small token from him in return. Legend has it that Houston scattered his carved wooden hearts all the way from Washington, D. C., to Texas. It is certainly true that Houston recruited men for the Texas army at the bar of Mrs. Long's tavern in Brazoria. Undoubtedly the first relationship was a casual one.

At the time the government officials fled to Harrisburg, thence to Galveston, to escape Santa Anna — and Houston was conducting the Runaway Scrape — Mrs. Long closed her tavern and retired to the Island City for the safety of herself and her family.

At the close of the Revolution she reopened her public house at Brazoria, which was but twelve miles from the capital of Columbia. From the time that the first Congress met and Houston was inaugurated President of the Republic, October 22, 1836, he was a familiar guest at Mrs. Long's establishment, sometimes alone and at other times with contemporaries. The names of the two were linked romantically and it is of record that Houston proposed marriage to her. Moreover, Mrs. Long was one of the popular widows that he continued to date after the capital was moved to Houston. An especially graceful dancer, she was said to have graced the President's soirees at the new capital upon his personal invitation.

Simultaneously Mirabeau B. Lamar, Houston's distant cousin, who had reached the Mexican province July 22, in time to share honors at San Jacinto, was apparently replacing him in the lady's affections. Although not the first of Mrs. Long's suitors in Texas, the controversial Lamar was the most persistent. Their relationship, chequered as it was, extended the length of sixteen years. The occasion of their first meeting was at an entertainment Mrs. Long gave for the New Orleans Greys, who were passing through the town en route to San Antonio, before the Alamo fell. Having heard that Lamar had come to Texas to join the Revolution, Mrs. Long invited the dashing widower and literary man to address the patriots.

In 1837 Mrs. Long opened the hotel in Richmond. Lamar, who had lived at the inn at Brazoria during his term as vice president under Houston, made Mrs. Long's Richmond hotel his headquarters during his successful campaign for the presidency from 1837 to 1838. Under Mrs. Long's inspiration Lamar began an ambitious writing program including the Long memoirs which he left incomplete. While the love affair was evidently flowering in 1838 Lamar proposed marriage and further committed himself in a poem entitled "Serenade:"

> The moon, the cold, chaste moon, my love,
> Is riding in the sky;
> And like a bridal veil, my love,
> The clouds are floating by.
> Oh, brighter than that planet, love,
> Thy face appears to me;
> But when shall I behold its light,
> Through bridal drapery?
>
> We owe our gratitude, my love,
> To Sol's enlivening ray;
> And yet I prize the moonlight, love,
> Above the glare of day.
> O bonnie Jane, thou art to me
> Whate'er in both is best —
> Thou art the moonbeam to mine eye,
> The sunbeam to my breast.

Lamar continued to pursue Mrs. Long after he won his campaign and occupied the capital at Austin. In fact, the friendship continued after a fashion until Lamar's marriage to Henrietta Maffit of Galveston in 1851.

There is no doubt that a warm friendship existed between Mrs. Long and Lamar. But it is doubtful that she took him as seriously as he did her. They were entirely disparate in personality. While he was a romanticist and a visionary unable to cope with reality, she was a forthright realist and highly successful. By 1841 Mrs. Long had liquidated Long's debts and her own and had acquired substantial property. The census of the Republic for the year 1840 listed Mrs. Long's taxable property as follows: 3,944 acres of land under a completed title (patent), three town lots in Richmond, 12 slaves, two horses, and 50 head of cattle (which meant she owned 75 as the number listed was in excess of an exemption of the first twenty-five neat or horned animals). By 1850 Mrs. Long's plantation in Richmond was one of sixteen in Texas whose average valuation was $20,000 — a sizable figure for the time. In addition to this, she occupied a leading role in the Republic and her legend continued to burgeon.

When the Civil War began in 1861 Mrs. Long — a well preserved matriarch at 63 — was a favorite citizen of Richmond. Greeted as "Aunt Jane" or "Grandma Long," she was loved by both blacks and whites impartially. Still beautiful, she was described by one of her contemporaries, Mrs. Elias Wightman, as "a remarkably handsome old lady, tall and erect, with bright dark eyes, an abundance of dark hair just sprinkled with grey, and a mouth and chin in which sweetness and firmness were singularly blended."

No longer the keeper of an inn, she was surrounded by second and third generation descendants and was noted for her graciousness. While her old boyfriend Sam Houston had retreated to his rocking chair in Huntsville to contemplate the futility of the war, Mrs. Long threw herself into the support of the Confederacy with abandon. She sewed and knitted assiduously to fill packages the Richmond ladies sent to the boys in grey, one of whom was her grandson, James Edward Winston.

In her unswerving loyalty to the South, Mrs. Long was simultaneously contributing to Texas — the cause for which she had lost both Long and Milam . . . that former Mexican province for which Austin had been imprisoned and for whom young Travis had made his stand at the Alamo . . . that Republic Houston, Lamar, and the patriot Thomas J. Rusk had validated at San Jacinto. From a territory of Spain, Jane Long had seen Texas become a Mexican frontier, had watched it emerge into a republic, then finally achieve annexation to the United States, and in 1861 become a member of the Confederate States of America. Within a quarter of a century, Mrs. Long had witnessed Texas declare its independence twice: from Mexico on March 2, 1836, and from the United States on March 2, 1861. By the time the last bugle call was sounded and the Confederate flag furled in 1865, Mrs. Long had not only witnessed more than half a century of American history unfold, beginning with the War of 1812 and proceeding through the struggle for Texas' independence, she had been a vital part of it.

Mrs. Long's contribution to the civilian aftermath of peace was no less dedicated. With her typical pioneer fortitude, she survived the harsh reconstruction period that ended in 1870. She was active in the period of development that began in that same year. At her side to assist her and direct the management of her extensive acreage was her grandson, the distinguished Colonel James Edward Winston — Civil War veteran, civic leader, and financier. The Texas heroine had come full circle. She had remained loyal to

Texas through three wars and numerous expeditions. She had lived to see the emergence of a new South. She had lived to hail the advent of a new nation.

And as she lived so did she die with characteristic stamina on December 30, 1880, at the age of eighty-two years and six months. Jane Wilkinson Long is buried at Richmond. Not far from her gravesite the Brazos still wends its way to the sea — that same sea to which the brave woman went down in ships piloted by stouthearted men who, like the fabled centaurs, came and passed and cast their shadows .

# Mary Austin Holley

MARY AUSTIN HOLLEY

# Mary Austin Holley

by
W. C. NUNN

She was the "first lady ambassador at large" for Texas and bore the name of Mary Austin Holley. This literary-minded first cousin of Stephen F. Austin entered life in New England on October 30, 1784. Her father, Elijah Austin, occupied a better than ordinary economic position. He was considered "well known to the mercantile community of New Haven and New York" and opened a new phase of American commerce with China in 1790. In this trade, he exchanged southern Pacific sealskins for Cantonese tea. Esther Phelps, Mary Austin Holley's mother, received an education "in the then only boarding school for young ladies in New England" before her marriage to Elijah Austin on November 7, 1776.

Mary Austin Holley, with five other children in the family, spent her childhood in comparative luxury at a large home in New Haven, Connecticut. "Cherry furniture — bureau and table — with easy chair and candlestand" adorned one room, according to the family records. The complete dining room nearby held two "cherry" sideboards, well provided with wines and cider, a "mahogany tea caddy," and a silver service that boasted a pair of sugar tongs. Opulence marked the "big parlor," for it was deemed a "magnificent apartment" with its books on the table, "prints with glasses" on the walls, and a rare Wilton carpet on the floor — or used in summer only, "the still rarer straw matting from China . . . the admiration of New Haven." A coat of arms, hanging on the mantel, lent dignity to the room. The house remained Mary's home as she attended New Haven schools, studying music and languages.

Mary had left the residence for the home of her uncle, Timothy Phelps, at the time of her marriage to Reverend Horace Holley on January 1, 1805. The groom, according to historian Mattie Austin Hatcher, was a recent graduate of Yale College where Horace Holley had been a disciple of Timothy Dwight, an elderly theological and metaphysical champion of Calvinism. Described as a "handsome, dark-haired young student," devout Holley spent four years at Yale. There he entered into the "polite circles of the town" and at singing societies, religious revivals, debating clubs, and gatherings "on the Green" he first met and then developed affection for Mary Austin. Eventually he persuaded her to become his wife, and the two moved to Greenfield, Connecticut, where he held a pastorate from 1805 until 1808.

There Mary lived contentedly in a cottage whose windows provided her with a view of the distant waters of Long Island Sound. Perhaps the outstanding event of this period was the visit to her from a "puny boy" ten or twelve years of age. The child was Stephen F. Austin, son of her uncle, Moses Austin. The homesick cousin, a student at Bacon Academy in Colchester, Connecticut, welcomed the opportunity to meet his charming relative as a tie to his kin, for he seriously missed the residence of his father in Upper Louisiana. As for Mary, she formed an attachment for young Austin that endured a separation of twenty-five years.

It was not long after this visit that Mrs. Holley urged her husband to leave Greenfield with its annual pastoral salary of $560. Mary felt that since their first child was soon to be born, that the time had come for the couple to rise above the subsistence level. Thus she encouraged Horace to accept a proffered position at Boston. The greatest field for usefulness apparently lay there, and this Mary believed to be "the first consideration of a Christian minister." So she rejoiced when Holley took the pastorate at Boston.

Mary went home to New Haven to await the birth of her daughter, Harriette Williman on December 13, 1808, and then she followed Horace on to Boston. The city, a literary center, provided ten happy years for her. During this period, Mrs. Holley came to reject the strongest beliefs of the early Puritans and instead contented herself in believing that "God was a God of love and not a merciless tyrant." "Religion," she found, "was destined not only to fit one for Heaven but to equip one for a richer life on earth." Her zest in living increased as she turned to literary, civic, and philanthropic pursuits. She found pleasure as well in the training of her young child, Harriette. But always she liked to travel, being "never so happy as when on the wing," and thus frequently Mrs. Holley visited her own and Dr. Holley's families at New Haven and Salisbury. She wrote of one of these journeys by steamboat in New York state:

> We are perfectly steady as in a house & have every accommodation that we possibly could have on shore. We cut rapidly through this river, wh. is as smooth as a mirror & the banks are highly picturesque. We pass by all the boats on the river. We have met 3 sloops loaded with soldiers & sailors on their way to the northern frontier. As soon as we came abreast they struck up their musick and gave three cheers each wh. were returned by the passengers. We have somewhere about 150 passengers, & an abundance of room, except at night, when the scene was truly amusing. *We* had taken our berths before hand, and had an opportunity of looking down upon our less comfortable fellow travelers below, who were stowed so thick that there was no place to step a foot between the sofas. We were all night taking in women & children, till

the ladies cabin was crammed.

There was no sleeping but it was a beautiful moonlight evening . . . & sublime thro my little window. I was determined not to lose a view of the highlands, rose as soon as the day began to dawn, when I had an opportunity of viewing the grand scenery at West Point. The views are the finest I have ever seen & it was not difficult to imagine ones' self among the stupendous cliffs & beautiful lakes of Scotland.

Later at home in Boston, Mary forgot joys of travel in unhappiness that came to her resulting from the effects of the austere faith of the Calvinists. Her pastor husband, Dr. Holley, at first popular in Boston when he believed that the "*liberals*" were in effect the "*licentious*" found in time that they possessed more kindliness than the orthodox — and, in truth, indicated "less of show and more of spirit." Holley discovered, to be his only authority, "The recognized will of God, ascertained equally from the written revelation and from the still clearer revelation, the works of nature." Soon thereafter he became a foremost liberal and boldly defended his ideas, making enemies where friends had been before. Finally, continued conflicts outweighted any joys that Holley found in pastoral work at Boston, and he decided to go elsewhere.

Dr. Horace Holley realized his expectations for a better position when he accepted his election to the presidency of Transylvania University at Lexington, Kentucky, in 1818. He began his journey in March and went by way of Philadelphia, Washington, Richmond, and Monticello. At Monticello, he made friends with Thomas Jefferson — the great liberal of his time. It was in April that Holley accepted the presidency at $3,000 a year, declaring that he could "form more minds there than any institution in New England." Besides, he found Lexington beautiful, its paved streets broad, clean, well shaded, and lined by houses mostly of brick that were "genteel and comfortable." Hospitality he discovered as well, and he breakfasted with Henry Clay at Ashland.

During Dr. Holley's absence in the South, Mary, still in Boston, welcomed the birth of her second child — a son. She named the infant Horace Austin Holley.

Soon after, Dr. Holley moved his family to Lexington, and Mary faced with hope her new responsibilities as a college president's wife. She welcomed visitors in the home and there entertained celebrities among whom were Marquis Lafayette, James Monroe, and General Andrew Jackson. For Lafayette, Mary composed an ode to be read before the welcoming ceremonies at Transylvania. She also hoped for some sort of financial endorsement for the college from the state legislature and wrote of the interest of Kentucky legislators in the school:

> We had last week a sort of *literary stir.* The Legislature at last consented to take into consideration the merits of the University, & sent up a committee of twenty. (It would have been well if the whole body had adjourned here) to inquire into its condition & its wants. These gentlemen, scarcely one of whom has ever drawn a literary breath before, after listening to a very sensible and polished address from the President, stating the nature, the prospects, & the claims of the Institution, appealing to their generous and their selfish feelings so as not to be resisted, they were carried for two days through all the exercises in the several departments of the languages, *belles lettres*, the lectures on medicine & chemistry, all of which were as new to them as if they had lived in the world before the Flood. Their astonishment at the *miracles of learning* was perfectly ludicrous. The sound of Latin & Greek, the wonders of chemistry, & that boys could be made orators, (for they attended a declamation) surprised them. They went away deeply impressed with the importance of the Institution, saying some of them, that they had learned more in a day than in their whole lives before, & it is expected that they will make a very favorable report to the *learned* body from which they were selected whether anything will be *done* remains to be determined. If this attempt to obtain an endorsement fail, it will not be for the lack of effort on the part of your brother. He [Dr. Horace Holley] will come off with a clear conscience in any event. He is becoming wonderfully popular — even the good ladies who trembled for the cause of orthodoxy are beginning to sing his praises. All of these have found out that they cannot pull him down, and they *may* pull themselves up by his means.

Two years passed quickly at Lexington, and in 1820, Mary began to look beyond the walls of Transylvania. She anticipated a visit to her brother, Horace Austin, who had gone westward to Missouri where he could be with their uncle, Moses Austin. Moses Austin, Mary knew, had been readying himself to push southwestward into the Spanish province of Texas. Adventurous at heart, she longed to hear all of the fascinating details of her uncle's plan for removing to Texas — a project realizable only if permission could be secured from the Spaniards who then controlled the territory.

Mary made no visit to her relatives in the West at that time. Still the next year, 1821, would prove an eventful one for the Austin family. Moses Austin died in June of that year, and his death occurred before he had been able to take advantage of the permission already granted him by the Spanish authorities to settle an Anglo-American colony in Texas. Strategic proved the year for Mexico who gained its independence from Spain in September and soon established a liberal government. The young nation invited into Texas all foreigners who had aided in the struggle for freedom. Before the year closed, Stephen F. Austin, Mrs. Holley's relative whom she recalled so fondly as her child visitor years back in Greenfield, led the first group of settlers into Texas. Thus he took up the work left by his father.

Mary Austin Holley's destiny lay elsewhere during these years. A Kentucky group, who almost from the time of Holley's arrival at Lexington had been on the alert to discover whether or not he was a "heretic," had become convinced that he held heretical ideas. They determined to compel Dr. Holley to resign. A Presbyterian minister issued two open letters that charged him with instructing unsoundly on matters of importance pertaining to "man's eternal welfare." The letter also sternly warned Dr. Holley that unless he resigned, a rival institution would be established at once.

Holley at first left all defense to friends who evidenced that the institution had progressed more during his leadership than in any past period "three times as long." This improvement had come despite a lack of adequate funds. Optimistic that the attacks on his religious convictions would soon cease, Dr. Holley visited the North. Mary Austin Holley, during the same period, took Harriette and little Horace — whose mental and physical condition caused her anxiety — to Newport, Kentucky, to visit briefly. Once back home, the attacks renewed. His critics branded Dr. Holley as being immoral and profane because he attended balls, the theater, and the races. Even a statue that Mary had placed in the drawing room received condemnation, because as she said, "It was not covered to the ears in an inky cloak, an ecclesiastic's surplice, or some other tasteless and unfitting garb." Charges of heresy and unfitness for instructing youth continued, while there was evidence at the same time that financial support for the university could not be obtained from the Legislature.

Dr. Holley, at length, yielded to pressure and resigned his office in March, 1827, nine years from the time he arrived at Lexington.

As 1821 had been an eventful year for the Austin family, so 1827 proved tragic for Mary Austin Holley. The Holleys moved southward toward Louisiana, hoping there to found a new school. On April 8, in route to New Orleans by steamboat, Mrs. Holley wrote to her married daughter, Harriette, at Lexington telling of forebodings that "intruded themselves into her apparently bright prospects." "When shall I see Kentucky again and what may not first intervene!" Still the great Mississippi somehow gave her courage for tasks that lay ahead.

The greater part of the Holley family income back in Lexington had come from certain wealthy Louisiana planters who placed their sons in the Holley home for individual care and instruction. So Horace and Mary projected the idea of establishing a school in New Orleans for such young men, where as a finishing touch, they would be taken to Europe on a conducted tour. There a broad view of European cultural contributions could be gained at first hand. Mrs. Holley hoped that such travel might prove of special benefit to her child, little Horace, who suffered from certain nervous defects and needed care which might be found only in Europe.

At New Orleans, citizens became enthusiastic over the plan for a school, but they argued against a European tour, feeling that an absence of a few years in cooler Europe would unfit their sons for the climate in Louisiana. Offers to raise ample funds came, and it was alleged that hundreds of young men were ready to enroll as soon as the school could be opened.

This was a dream never to be. New Orleans in July did little to help the health of Dr. Horace Holley which was already weakened by work and worry at Transylvania. In desperation, he found the "ever-smiling, violet scented South, alluring but to destroy." Dr. Holley begged instead for but "one breath of air from the northern shore of Freedom."

Mary yielded to his pleadings and arranged to sail for New York on the *Louisiana*, a packet then in port. But once on the high seas, disease stalked the vessel as storm beset it. Yellow fever seized its fiery hold upon both Mary and her invalid husband as the *Louisiana* also fought for its life in a tropical hurricane. Poor Mrs. Holley, who could have given him careful nursing had she not been stricken herself, lay helpless as his condition worsened. Mary knew by the smell of burning tar the dreadful nature of the disease and then realized, in torture shortly after, that he had gone. Later she could hear the crew as they slowly lowered the body of her husband into the surging waters. In her agony, Mary could still declare: "I will love the sea, because it is his tomb."

Back in New England Mrs. Holley went to the region that awakened memories of her youth. Still there was to be no time lost upon sentiment, for she immediately took up the task of preparing a memoir that Mary vowed would place Dr. Horace Holley's name "above the slanders of the malevolent." She organized biographical and explanatory notes which were then gathered together as an appendix and published with *A Discourse on the Genius and Character of the Reverend Horace Holley*, earlier written and delivered by Dr. Charles Caldwell of Transylvania.

Briefly Mrs. Holley became a saleswoman and went to Washington to find subscribers for the book which had gone into print in 1828. Succeeding there, she turned southward to Lexington both for a visit with her daughter, Harriette, and to plan the future.

Mary had not yet decided what to do for a living, when she accepted the invitation of two of her friends, Mr. and Mrs. Hermagene Labranche to visit them on their plantation near New Orleans. She left Horace temporarily with Harriette, and after a week's visit, Mrs. Holley wrote enthusiastically:

> They received me with great kindness and I enjoy here the repose and leisure my mind requires, I find it in every way delightful and if it was not for you and Horace, I would spend my life here. The orange trees are in flower and the mocking birds are singing all around me . . . . It would be my own fault if I were not happy. Mr. Labranche has

> imported from London a first rate piano, the tones are finer than I ever heard. It is of cabinet form and of rosewood. They could not have suited my taste better. I give Melazie lessons every day and we have music all the time.

Mary soon accepted an invitation to remain with Mr. and Mrs. Lebranche as a governess to Melazie, their daughter. Horace was brought from Harriette's home in Kentucky. Mary had two adopted homes, both possessions of the Labranche family — one on a Louisiana sugarcane plantation and the other in New Orleans on St. Pierre Street. She wrote, on November 28, 1829, describing the beauty of the sugar plantation:

> If you could in a moment be transported to this place you would think yourself in a terrestrial paradise, for it is indeed more like one than any place I have been in and made on me on arriving the liveliest impression . . . . If you wish to know what luxurious living is, you must come here. It does not consist of the quantity of things but in their variety and delicacy and exact arrangement. The roses and geraniums are still blooming and the beauty of the orange trees exceeds my imagination . . . . I commence my school on Monday, choosing not to give myself too much time for reflection. Besides Melazie, I have two little Browns, Euphemie and Adeline. They are all alacrity, & Horace is ashamed to be outdone by them.

In another letter to Harriette, written on January 1, 1830, she told of the celebration attending the end of the harvesting of the sugar. Of this event held on the Labranche plantation she wrote:

> I don't know what the religionists of Lexington would have thought of the ushering in of this holy day here. The sugar is finished and the Negroes had a holiday . . . . They had a beef killed . . . and plenty of wine and good cheer. In gratitude to their master and to celebrate the occasion they came up in procession — with every sort of noisy instrument of their own manufacturing in the way of music . . . violins, kettle drums, tambourines, and triangle made their bow and sang with great glee. There was the Congo dancer, the Senegal, and the *Americaine*, some very old Congo men performed with great agility coming up to their master on one knee, then on the other . . . with other exhibitions of homage, all in time to the music.

Opportunity came for Mary to travel again. Madame Labranche desired to visit her son, Nemese, a student in a northern school, but she spoke only French. Mary thus became her interpreter with the same salary she had received as governess. As the Labranches were in route home, Mrs. Holley visited Harriette at Lexington briefly, and then she too returned to the Louisiana plantation.

But there she became restless. Mrs. Holley felt that she must have new friends and adventure if she were to live a full life. Besides, Mary missed Horace whom she had placed in a school in Kentucky, hoping that the discipline offered there might provide the means of overcoming his nervous infirmities. Mrs. Holley wanted her own home, where she herself could give him the attention and training he needed. Mary began to dream of a home in Texas.

Henry Austin, Mrs. Holley's brother, had but recently located in Texas, and this strange new land to the West fascinated her. She wrote both to Henry and to her cousin, Stephen F. Austin, foremost colonizer of the Anglo-Americans there. Mary's letters concerned possibilities which she had been considering of gathering the family about her in Texas.

Stephen F. Austin, pleased to hear from his charming relative, made arrangements to reserve land for her on Galveston Bay. So it was that Mary visited the Austin colony in October, 1831. She wrote, as a result of this visit, *Texas*, with the by-line "Observations, Historical, Geographical and Descriptive, in a Series of Letters Written during a Visit to Austin's Colony, with a view to a permanent settlement in that country, in the Autumn of 1831." The book was published at Baltimore in 1833, and its announcement declared it as "being the first book published in English on Texas."

"To the enterprising public, especially to emigrants, the following letters in the hope of being useful, are respectfully presented." Thus Mary Austin wrote in her introduction. To those not so enterprising she warned: "The idle and the vicious, as it happens every where, will be sure to be disappointed in Texas. Like the hero of Milton, such characters carry their discontent with them." Emigrants in Texas would have to expect to work if they developed the true agricultural potentialities of the region. Thus Mary wrote:

> A soil that yields the fruits of nearly every latitude, almost spontaneously, with a climate of perpetual summer, must, like that of other countries, have a seedtime and a harvest. Though the land be, literally flowing with milk and honey, yet, the cows must be milked, and the honey must be gathered. Houses must be built and enclosures made. The deer must be hunted, and the fish must be caught. From the primeval curse, that, in the sweat of his brow, man shall eat bread, though its severity be mollified, there is no exception, even here. The emigrant should bear in mind, that in a new community, labour is the most valuable commodity . . . . He is, abundantly, furnished, with raw materials, but his hands must mould them into the forms of art.

There were twelve of her letters from Austin's colony published in this volume which closed with an appendix of two parts. The first portion dealt with "Questions Relative to Texas," while the second, of an entirely different nature, was titled "Communication from San Felipe de Austin Relative to the Events in Texas, 1832." This second portion indicated, through official statements by leading Texans, how the people there "had been provoked, by several illegal and tyrannical acts of the military officers of the general government." Mary further explained that these same communications "hailed with joy the success of Gen. Santa Anna's party." Santa Anna had just come into power as president of Mexico, and it seemed — although the assumption later proved false — that he offered a "pledge of more just and liberal administration of the general government."

Her letters tell of Mary's passage on October 19, 1831, to Texas in the *Spica*, a vessel small enough to cross a "troublesome bar" at the mouth of the Brazos River. Mrs. Holley reached the Texas coast in three days and then went at once up to Bolivar at the head of navigation on the Brazos River near San Felipe and but fifteen miles from Galveston Bay. She told of her approach to Bolivar and described its environs:

> Before sun-set I arrived at this my forest home, for such Bolivar may now be regarded, being the place of my temporary abode in Texas. Bolivar, though selected as an advantageous location for a commercial town, and laid off for that purpose before Brazoria, at present consists of but a single residence . . . . The land, in about Bolivar, is the best in the colony; clothed with heavy timber, with peach and cane undergrowth, to the distance of six miles from the river. The bank of the river in front of the town, is a high bluff of stiff red clay. About fifty acres are cleared and under cultivation. The undergrowth of the best land in the Brazos valley is cane and a species of laurel, the leaves of which taste like the kernel of the peach stone, containing an extraordinary quantity of prussic acid. The leaves resemble those of the peach tree. Hence it is called by the colonists, wild peach. This tree is regarded as certain indication of the best soil. Hence, when a colonist wishes to describe his land as first rate, he says it is *all peach and cane land.*

Mary mentioned briefly the most important Anglo-American settlement in Texas and its originator, Stephen F. Austin:

> The town of San Felipe de Austin was founded in 1824 by Col. Austin and the commissioner of the government, Baron de Bastrop. It is the capital of Austin's Colony, situated on the right bank of the Brazos river, eighty miles from the gulf by land, and one hundred and eighty miles by the meanders of the river. The site of the town is exceedingly beautiful. It is a high prairie bluff, which strikes the river at the upper or northern limit of the level region. It is the residence of the Empresario, Col. Austin. The state and municipal officers of the jurisdiction hold their offices here, and here all the land and judicial business of the colony is transacted.

Mary said of Stephen F. Austin who was then not yet forty years of age that "through the hardships of his life" that he "looks much older than he really is." Then she rightly predicted:

> When in the progress of years, the state of Texas shall take her place among the powerful empires of the American continent, her citizens will doubtless regard Col. Austin as their patriarch, and children will be taught to hold his name in reverence; for though there have been many other respectable men engaged in the work of colonization, yet Col. Austin began the work, and was the first to open the wilderness. All the subsequent labour of others has been comparatively easy.

Mary had written all of the twelve letters composing the manuscript in the month of December, 1831. She found one's feelings in Texas as being "unique and original, and very like a dream or youthful vision realized." And in her last letter of the book, she added with a touch of eloquence:

> Here, as in Eden, man feels alone with the God of nature, and seems, in a peculiar manner, to enjoy the rich bounties of heaven, in common with all created things. The animals, which do not fly from him; the profound stillness; the genial sun and soft air, — all are impressive, and are calculated, both to delight the imagination, and to fill the heart, with religious emotions.

Too soon the time came to leave her brother Henry Austin's residence at Bolivar and return to the Labranche family in Louisiana. The *Spica* had come back to Texas, and so the same vessel carried her eastward to New Orleans. It was Christmas morning when she waved goodbye to her cousin, Stephen F. Austin. His figure appeared "slight" when in "full relief" against the sky. She knew that his health was poor, and she feared she was never to see him again. Mary realized too that ahead of him lay the arduous journey to Saltillo, for he had been named to represent Texas in the state legislature which would convene there.

Once more in Louisiana, Mrs. Holley returned to her teaching, for there was much Melazie Labranche must learn before the girl's course of study could be completed. So it was Mary's brother, Charles, a teacher and also the rector of St. Thomas Church near Baltimore, Maryland, who obtained at that city an acceptance of her manuscript *Texas* by Armstrong and Plaskett.

Pleased over the knowledge that the book would be published, Mary was more directly concerned with the training of her son Horace. He evidenced a nervous disability throughout his childhood that continued into youth. Still Mrs. Holley indicated delight in "his tractability," his joy in fishing, hunting, and gardening. She wrote Harriette that "I am sure there must be something in Horace's brain if one but could get it out. I yet hope to succeed in making something of him . . . . He is quite the gallant with our *jeunes Parisiennes* who can not speak or understand a word of English. At other times he sings Jim Crow, & gives very good imitations of camp meeting preaching, much to their amusement."

The cholera began striking down hundreds in New Orleans and scores too along the Mississippi River. Servants who served at night sometimes were dead by morning. "Instead of the usual gay *bon jour*, the family met in tears and dismay, not knowing where the pestilence would end." Horace fell victim first, and then Mary, after nursing him to recovery, contracted the disease. "I was myself seized with spasms after I had gone to bed. I felt the circulation arrested and coldness fast spreading over me like the chill of death . . . . At this instant I heard the Doctor, who never left us." Mrs. Holley detailed the physician's treatment, writing, "He ran up and gave me ether, peppermint, & hot brandy toddy & with my feet in the fire, and a hot flat-iron which happened to be there (thanks to my patchwork) at my breast, & friction of the hands, after keeping the Doctor and Madam Hermogene with me the greatest part of the night, I went quietly to bed again."

Cholera stalked through Texas as well, and there her brother, Henry Austin, lost his wife and daughter in 1832. Yet he still, for a time at least, attempted to make a home for his motherless children at Bolivar. Mary, her health regained, could not go to him in his grief, for teaching duties in Louisiana and responsibilities to Horace detained her.

These two restraints proved but temporary. Melazie Labranche's education had been finished in Louisiana by the fall of 1833. Then too by December of that year, Mrs. Holley had arranged for Horace to go soon to Guatemala "with Mr. Savage, a disciplinarian of the old school," who believed that the young man's derangement had grown out of "his mother's indulgence." Thus free from these responsibilities, Mrs. Holley faced the possibilities of a new life at Lexington with Harriette — or another career in Texas with Austin relatives — or even a new possibility entirely — that of a romance. Of this she wrote to Harriette: "What would you say were I to tell you of another project — that I have half promised myself to Mr. Savage? But don't be frightened before you are hurt. There is nothing settled." Mary did not elaborate in detail but added:

> He has gone to Guatemala & will not return before July . . . . You do not know Mr. S. I never knew him well till now. I see in him much to respect and admire. He takes an interest in Horace, & is just what he requires — being at once decided, firm, amiable, and kind. You must keep my secret until I see how matters go, for after all — *je ne sais pas* . . . . Farewell, I hope something will occur to decide me quick.

She waited for a time in Louisiana for Mr. Savage who still had plans for Horace in Guatemala, but Mrs. Holley wrote nothing about romance. She had disposed of the first consignment of her book advantageously, and desired to return to Bolivar in pursuit of material for a second edition on Texas — or perhaps to write an entirely new volume. Still the question of whether to remain in Louisiana — turn toward Texas — or return to Lexington was settled for her by different hands.

A letter came from her brother, Henry Austin, in Texas which decided her actions. He wrote that political and financial conditions were so unstable and epidemics of cholera and other fevers so frequent that he determined to remove his children to a safer place — certainly for a year or two at least. Later he would return them to Texas when things stabilized. Mary immediately replied with an offer to make a home for his five motherless children at Lexington, if he would furnish her with $1,000 annually for their and her support. This, Mary wrote, was cheaper than he could place them elsewhere with the same advantages which she could provide.

Thus Mary postponed "her active career of happiness." Her thoughts were often with Texas and Stephen F. Austin. Austin had gone to Mexico City, sent by a convention held at San Felipe in 1833. His delegated purpose was to obtain separation of Texas from Coahuila and the repeal of an anti-Anglo-American immigration law. Repeal he obtained but not separation. Austin was arrested at Saltillo, on his way home, in January, 1834, under suspicion of trying to incite insurrection in Texas. He was returned to Mexico City. There Austin was imprisoned, being shifted from prison to prison until December, 1834, when he was released on bond although confined to the area of the federal district. Austin was eventually freed by a general amnesty law in July, 1835, and returned to Texas by way of New Orleans.

Mary Austin Holley's *Texas*, "Observations, Historical, Geographical, and Descriptive in a Series of Letters" or more recently titled *Letters from Texas* had been read by Stephen F. Austin during his imprisonment, but the volume was also studied by Santa Anna, dictator of Mexico. The Mexican leader examined a copy of the book that had fallen into his hands, and from it, learned of the defenseless condition of the colonists.

Mary herself set up a residence in Lexington, Kentucky, for the Henry Austin children but was back in Texas by May, 1835. She limited her stay to a few months, living during that time at her brother's home. But Henry Austin again determined that his children must resume living outside of Texas, as political conditions in that area continued to be insecure, while cholera too once more threatened. Thus Mary returned to the United States and was in Lexington before the summer ended. Still she turned her efforts in behalf of Texas, and events there proved the need of her aid.

Stephen F. Austin, in route home following his liberation, wrote her from New Orleans. He warned Mrs. Holley to prepare for an inevitable conflict in Texas. She could do this by rushing armed immigrants to the region. Texas, he foresaw, must be Americanized and made "an outwork on the West" to defend the "Key of the Western World — the mouths of the Mississippi River." He continued:

> The political importance of Texas to the great Western world, from the influence it may one day have on Louisiana, is so great, that it cannot fail to have due weight on all reflecting men and on Genl. Jackson and the Senate, in particular . . . . I wish a great immigration this fall and winter from Kentucky and Tennessee, *everywhere* . . . *anyhow*. For fourteen years I have had a hard time of it, but nothing shall daunt my courage or abate my exertions to complete the main object of my endeavors — to Americanize Texas. This fall and winter will fix our fate — a great immigration will settle the question.

Austin beseeched her to arouse the sympathies of the American people to the Texas cause. But the letter depressed Mrs. Holley, as she suddenly felt personally responsible for the dangers threatening there. She believed that through her book she had unconsciously played a part in stirring trouble. And thus she wrote:

> I little anticipated . . . I should one day become the historian of a Nation, or the biographer of him who brought it into being. I am an Austin. The motives which impelled me, and the impressions I received have been made public in the Letters to a distant brother making the first book ever published on the subject of Texas. Until that time . . . that beautiful country was a *Terra Incognita.*
>
> I have since had my doubts whether my over-haste to display to the enterprising world the blessings which a true and practical philanthropist had been for years quietly providing for them was really an advantage to the Country, since it was the means of hurrying over from the United States together with many excellent persons, a goodly proportion of her most restless population. Full of pretensions and overflowing with *patriotism*, often the veriest *demagoguery* . . . [They] forgot the genius and habits of the Mexican people; their newness of self government.

There was no time to reflect on the past — with a present so filled with crisis. Mary wrote her brother John and other relatives in New York, urging them to turn their efforts toward the Texas cause. John Austin answered his sister at once, assuring her that excitement there in behalf of Texas was intense with meetings being held to raise both volunteers and funds. He added that at least a half dozen armed vessels had left for the Texas coast.

John Austin concluded thusly: "It was rumored that President Jackson would not interfere so long as the Law of the Nations was not openly violated in sending men and supplies across the border."

Henry Austin declared in a letter to Mrs. Holley that he, out of his own pocket, had raised volunteers. He even sent to the front one of his own tenants and then gave his best horse and pistols to another whom he instructed to join the "Colorado Reserves" should the invaders successfully pass the first lines of defense at Goliad and San Antonio. Shortly after this letter, Henry left for New Orleans to raise money and provisions, and he wrote again from there, telling Mary of the fall of the Alamo. Henry Austin ended his painful message on an optimistic note: "I have no fear for the issue."

His guarded optimism proved to be warranted. He had mentioned in his letter that "The people have now taken the defense of the country into their own hands & marched almost en masse with their rifles to shoot down every Mexican they can find." These same people, under General Sam Houston, won on April 21, 1836, a decisive battle on the banks of the San Jacinto River. On April 25, Houston, as Commander in Chief of the Army, wrote David G. Burnet, President of the recently created Republic of Texas:

> "The conflict lasted about eighteen minutes from the time of the close action, until we were in possession of the enemy's encampment, taking one piece of cannon, (loaded), four stands of colours, all their camp equippage, stores and baggage."

Santa Anna himself was captured the day after the battle — disguised as a private soldier. The victory at San Jacinto could not atone for the fall of the Alamo, but it did secure independence for Texas.

Mary Austin Holley, living in the pleasant atmosphere of quiet Lexington, still sought to forward the victory. Of these endeavors, she wrote:

> We had an overflowing Meeting last night . . . . I made up a party of ladies . . . and never was I so complimented — never so proud. And who do you think was the orator? The new Commissioner from Texas Col. Lewis . . . . He gave a very clear exposition of Texas affairs . . . . Some excellent resolutions and a Memorial to Congress prepared by Mr. Martin passed unanimously with great applause.

About the same time, Mrs. Holley authored a stirring appeal, published in the *Lexington Intelligencer* of April 26, inviting the ladies of the city to call at her home and sew for the benefit of the "holy cause of Texas." Twice a week such meetings were held, and the materials for the uniforms of the volunteers were furnished by the gentlemen of Lexington.

Mary concentrated on the preparation of *Texas*, a new manuscript, not in letter form, narrating once more the history of the area. The book included some of the content of *Letters from Texas* – but was more comprehensive and gave extensive details occuring after 1831, when the first manuscript was prepared. Mrs. Holley divided the volume into fourteen chapters, the first three of which dealt with geography. Trade, natural history, towns, social life, Indians, and religion all received separate treatments. There were those chapters too dealing with money, colonization, government, and laws. The two final chapters were concerned with a "History of Gen. Austin and his Colony" and an account of the events of the revolution – bringing the history contained up to the date of publication.

The book appeared on the market in the summer of 1836, and the *Lexington Intelligencer* predicted with some truth:

> This work will be more valuable to emigrants than any that has yet been published as Mrs. Holley has not only been a resident of Texas but from her connection with individuals at the head of affairs in that country, has access to facts and documents which have not been equally at the command of other writers on the subject.

Mary Austin Holley had reason to be proud of her work. *Texas* continued to receive favorable notices. A review published at Cincinnati on August 3, 1836, declared:

> This is a much more systematic and important effort than the *Letters.* The details are more minute and copious, and the contents more comprehensive . . . . It will be perceived that Mrs. Holley's pen has lost none of its sprightliness and grace. She is an agreeable writer, adorning every subject and adding an interest to the dryest details. The work is complete, omitting nothing that the emigrant or the mere curious inquirer would wish to know.

In Texas, Mary excelled in her descriptions of the geography of the area. With an easy charm, she gave an accurate view of the rivers of the region, its bays, its prairies and woodlands. Yet Mrs. Holley could never quite restrain her enthusiasm for Texas and wrote of its climate:

> But while we claim nothing unreal, no poetic exaggeration, or fictitious excellence for this region, we would confidently assert, that no state on the continent is more iminently favored by nature, in fertility of soil and salubrity of climate than Texas, or presents a like combination of natural advantages.

Mary described the state of society in this manner:

> Every body's house is open, and table spread to accommodate the traveller; the best of every thing is presented freely, not indeed with the refinement and courtesy of a polished European community, but with the honest, blunt, but hearty welcome of a Texas backwoodsman. There are a few here of the higher class, whose manners are more courtly but not less sincere. Nature has lavished her treasures upon all, and they seem imbued with the spirit of liberality which such abundance should create. The poor and the rich, to use the correlatives where distinction there is none, get the same quantity of land on arrival; and if they do not continue equal, it is for want of good management on the one part, or superior industry and sagacity on the other. All are happy, because busy; and none meddle with the affairs of their neighbors, because they have enough to do to take care of their own. They are bound together, by a common interest, by sameness of purpose and hopes.

Outside of her book's success, Mrs. Holley suffered difficulties late in 1836. Henry Austin, still in Texas, had been unable to raise funds for the support of his children, although he struggled desperately to do so. Mary still cared for them in Lexington, and she badly needed the income from him. To provide funds for the family's maintenance, she sold a league of her property in Texas to a buyer "with the understanding that he might locate his land on any of a number of choice tracts." But according to Mrs. Holley, the buyer proved to be such a "screwing" fellow that Henry was finally compelled to let him have one of his own Brazos River tracts. This unhappy incident cooled slightly the warm regard between Mary and her brother and was but a step toward an eventual separation destined to occur. Then personal tragedy grieved Mrs. Holley late in December. Stephen F. Austin died at his home in Texas of pneumonia at age forty-three. Austin, the true father of the Anglo-American colonization movement in Texas, had been defeated in the election of September, 1836, for the presidency of the Republic of Texas. He subsequently accepted the offer of secretary of state and was seeking recognition of Texas independence by the United States at the time of his death.

In 1837, Mary continued to worry over Henry Austin's inability to raise funds. He declared that the Texas land fever had vanished. Despite Henry's pessimism, Mrs. Holley made a quick trip to New Orleans where she sold enough lands to meet her immediate financial needs. There she also arranged for Horace's return from Guatemala, and soon after placed him in school at Lexington.

Mary held other lands in Texas that Stephen F. Austin, years before, had helped her obtain. She hoped to sell enough of these lands to pay all her debts and keep the remainder for a future home.

December found Mrs. Holley back in Texas and, on Christmas Eve of

1837, she wrote from the town of Houston of having been in the company of President Sam Houston:

> Sunday night 24 — attended church in the Capitol. Visited the gallery of paintings escorted by the President, who dines with us every day. We stay in the boat & hold levee all the time. There is a rumour of the Mexicans upon our frontier. Don't be alarmed — means nothing. Start day after tomorrow for the Brazos on horseback 60 miles. The [land] office opens in January.
>
> . . .The main street of this city of a year extends from the landing into the prairie — a beautiful plain of some six miles wide, & extending, with points and islands of timber, quite to the Brazos. On this main street are two large hotels, 2 stories with galleries (crowded to overflowing) several stores 2 stories — painted white — one block of eleven stores (rent $500 each) — some 2 story dwelling houses — & then the capitol — 70 feet front — 140 rear — painted peach blossom about 1/4 mile from the landing.

Other correspondence to daughter Harriette told of the "rumors of the Mexicans on our borders." But "the alarm from the Frontier turns out to be — a marauding party for horses — warlike preparations go on." From Brazoria, she wrote on New Year's day: "We had a gay supper last night and danced in the new year, though being Sunday, we did not dance out the old—" Later at New Orleans, on her return route toward Lexington, she wrote on May 13, 1838:

> I have plenty of money, but in Texas currency & must be exchanged. It is par with Mississippi paper & rising. As soon as the loan [bill] passes the Texian Congress, which we shall hear next vessel, it will be better than any paper. Brother Henry came along with us to attend to business, & all will be right.

But all was not right, and Mary's financial condition had so worsened by late 1838, she despaired of immediate relief. Totaling her monies, she wrote: "On hand — $400.00. Query, what shall I do next?" Her dreams for selling Texas lands for railroad development had come to nothing.

Henry Austin, feeling the effects of the financial panic begun the year before, was completely discouraged. He had planned upon placing his children in school in New England after selling more lands. He even braved the Atlantic to the British Isles where he proposed the development of commercial operations in Texas. But rumors of a further invasion from Mexico reached England where all loans were stopped. Henry Austin then returned to Texas hoping to save the land he had there. Sadly he wrote Mary: "No more traveling on expenses . . . . My children can not suffer more than their father does and has most of his life—"

Mary's close friendship with Henry ended shortly after. No longer could she hope to share her "brother's fortunes." She visited her brother Charles, in Maryland, and other relatives as well during this period of financial difficulty. But good news came soon, for Mary learned that deep water had been discovered at the western end of Galveston Island. This knowledge might enable Mrs. Holley to sell her lands at a profit.

With visions of land sales before her eyes, Mary re-entered Texas in November, 1840. She also hoped for a home there. Mrs. Holley wrote Harriette, who was still in Lexington, that one of her acquaintances had sold land near hers for two dollars an acre. "I shall be able to do better than that elsewhere," she confided.

Also in the letter Mrs. Holley zestfully told of the voyage from New Orleans:

> We . . . came down the "shining River" between shores of waving cane . . . glistening in the sunshine. Then came the moon. It was glorious.
>
> Well, the next night before 12 we were at the Galveston Bar, but bright as the moon was the captain would not pass till day, & we played off & on. I could hardly dress before they were ready to land. We were but 32 hours. It seemed like magic — & the land truly like fairy land. The boat is so beautiful I could think of nothing but Cleopatra as I lay in my luxurious couch of the finest & whitest — resting from the fatigue of running about New Orleans.

Her plans miscarried once more. Mary returned to Lexington without any land profits, without making a new home in Texas, and without even seeing her brother, Henry. Still her innate enthusiasm would not die, and believing that "beams of the sun would shine upon her to the end," she yet planned for a home in the republic of the lone star. And thus it was that Mrs. Holley returned in 1843 to the region she loved so well. This time for a year's visit to Texas — but there was never to be a home for her there. Instead she met frustration, thwarting new dreams of writing a biography of Stephen F. Austin. Mrs. Holley had no opportunity to visit Peach Point plantation where Austin once lived and where he left essential records of his work. Still President Sam Houston and former President Mirabeau Lamar both urged her to write the book, and associates of Stephen F. Austin all willingly gave her interviews. So despite obstacles, Mary determined "to bring out his name from the rubbish that surrounded it in bright relief before the country." Hopefully, she returned to Lexington in the spring of 1844 with certain materials in hand.

The biography, like a home for Mrs. Holley in Texas, was never to be. Illness in route to Lexington weakened her strength. Then she found William

Brand, her son-in-law and Harriette's husband, quite ill when she arrived in Kentucky. Mary believed that Horace and she but added to Harriette's burdens, so in 1845, Mrs. Holley decided to return to teaching for the Labranche family where she knew her work would be welcomed.

Mary readapted herself to Louisiana plantation life at once. She began teaching music to the wife of Nemese Labranche and English to his little daughter. Then Mary received an urgent invitation from Mrs. Donatien Augustin, the former Melazie Labranche, to come to New Orleans and become an instructor for her small children. But at New Orleans there was still no opportunity for writing her biography of Stephen F. Austin.

Tragedy was not far away from her, and shortly after moving to the Augustin home, Mrs. Holley received the news of the death of William Brand. In her grief, Mary felt that she must remain strong for the sake of Harriette but that all the "swan's feathers had been plucked from the fan of her early fancy, and that only eagle feathers remained, for there was courage, and to spare for the long journey."

Mary herself died the next year. In July 1846, the *Picayune*, a newspaper of New Orleans, warned that yellow fever had appeared in epidemic proportions. But warnings could not protect, and Mary with her "eagle feathers" of courage, lacked at sixty-two the strength of the young widow of Dr. Horace Holley who had survived the disease during another summer in 1827. And so it was on August 2, 1846, that the end came but shortly after she had exclaimed deliriously: "I see worlds upon worlds rolling in space. Oh it is wonderful."

# Suzanna Dickinson

SUZANNA DICKINSON

# Suzanna Dickinson

by
DAYTON KELLEY

For thirteen days the siege had continued and now all the defenders were dead. The Alamo had fallen!

Forth from its rubble, walking resolutely, a child clutched to her breast and followed closely by a Mexican soldier, came a young woman who had experienced, with the defenders, every hour of that two-week-long siege. Among the slain defenders was her husband, Almaron Dickinson who had commanded the meager artillery which had played such an important role in holding off the Mexican Army attacking the fortress.

She had last seen him when the battle was at its heighth. He had found her in a small room near the chapel and had informed her that the attackers were inside the walls. A quick embrace, a few words and he was gone, back to his post with the defenders.

Now she was on her way with their child, to an audience with General Antonio Lopez de Santa Anna, the self-styled "Napoleon of the West," who had sent one of his officers to look for her. She would learn later that her friend Mrs. Ramon Musquiz, with whom she had stayed before the siege began, had interceded in her behalf with the Mexican general.

Those days with the Musquiz family now seemed so long ago and so unreal that she wondered if they had really ever happened. She and her husband, with their daughter, little more than a year old, had come to San Antonio with several other Texians from Gonzales when it was learned that Santa Anna at the head of a large Mexican Army was on his way into Texas. For several days Suzanna and the child Angelina had stayed in the home of the Musquiz family, but on the day the Mexican Army was sighted on the outskirts of San Antonio, Almaron had taken them inside the fortress to be near him.

This was not the first time Almaron had offered his services as a soldier. He had been an artilleryman in the army before they were married and since coming to Texas in 1831 had been on hand to participate in at least two momentous events. At Gonzales the previous October, he had been among the Texans who refused to give up the cannon loaned to the colonists by the Mexican government for protection against the Indians. Colonel Ugartechea, in command of the Mexican forces at San Antonio, had sent for the cannon and when the colonists gathered to protest, a sharp conflict had ensued and the Mexicans had retreated to San Antonio.

A few weeks later some of those same men from Gonzales were among the Texans who laid seige to San Antonio and drove the Mexicans out, forcing them to cross the Rio Grande into Mexico. One of the men from Gonzales was Almaron Dickinson who put his skill with artillery to work and built a carriage for the lone cannon possessed by the Texans.

The Dickinsons had come to Texas from Tennessee. It was said that the two had been in love, but they had quarrelled and Almaron had become engaged to one of Suzanna's best friends. Suzanna had been asked to be a bridesmaid and Almaron had been sent to escort her to the wedding. The couple, after talking things over, eloped that night and had come to Texas where Almaron had become a blacksmith at Gonzales.

While the Texans under William B. Travis and James Bowie fortified the Alamo, Suzanna and Angelina had stayed in the Musquiz home and Mrs. Musquiz and Suzanna had become fast friends. Ramon Musquiz was the political chief of Bexar and although he had declared his support of Santa Anna, he was friendly to the Texans. His wife had taken a special liking to Suzanna Dickinson and it was to the Musquiz home that Almaron had galloped on his horse the day the Mexican Army was sighted and had whisked Suzanna and Angelina into the Alamo. Those in the Musquiz house had seen him racing down the street at breakneck speed and had heard him say as he reigned to a stop near the door "Quick, Sue, the Mexicans are upon us! Give me the babe and jump on behind me!" She had handed up the child, mounted behind him and they had headed for the fortress.

There they found several other women already inside. All were wives or relatives of men from San Antonio who had joined the Texans in their fight against Santa Anna. Suzanna was the only woman present from the States.

Once inside the Alamo, Suzanna could not help but notice the flurry of activity. Men everywhere were readying the defenses, working with the cannon, and taking stock of food and ammunition supplies. Bullets were to be molded, a water supply to be assured, and weapons to be cleaned and made ready.

Colonel Travis was already writing messages informing other Texans of the arrival of the Mexican Army and asking for men and supplies. "We have 150 men and are determined to defend the Alamo to the end," he wrote to the mayor of Gonzales. Selecting as couriers John W. Smith and Dr. John Sutherland, he sent them off with instructions to tell others that he would fire a signal cannon three times each day to let them know that the Alamo still resisted.

One of Santa Anna's first acts was to unfurl from the tower of San Fernando Church a huge red banner — the signal of no quarter! And one of the first acts of the Texans, as Travis put it one of his message, was to answer "with a cannon shot." There was no doubt in Suzanna's mind that Almaron had gleefully participated in this act of defiance.

As the garrison in the Alamo settled down to the routine of waiting and watching for the reinforcements which Travis had appealed for, but which never came, Suzanne took up the burden of looking after little Angelina and spending as much time as possible with her husband. He was everywhere looking to the artillery emplacements — an 18-pounder here, two 12-pounders there, a parapet to be built somewhere else, and a battery to be installed on the roof of the church. Suzanna never knew when he might be called upon for advice or counsel.

There was cooking to be done for the men of the garrison and the wounded and ill to be looked after. The men lacked nothing in the way of food for there were enough provisions to last for a month if necessary.

On February 24th Travis sent out two more messengers with an appeal for help. Addressed "To the people of Texas and all Americans in the World," the message went directly to Sam Houston:

> —Fellow Citizens and Compatriots: I am besieged . . . I have sustained a continual Bombardment and cannonade for 24 hours and have not lost a man. The enemy has demanded a surrender at discretion, otherwise, the garrison are to be put to the sword, if the fort is taken. I have answered the demand with a cannon shot, and our flag still waves proudly from the walls. I shall never surrender or retreat. Then, I call upon you in the name of Liberty, of patriotism, and every thing dear to the American character, to come to our aid with all dispatch. The enemy is receiving reinforcements daily and will no doubt increase to three or four thousand in four or five days. If this call is neglected, I am determined to sustain myself as long as possible and die like a soldier who never forgets what is due his own honor and that of his country. VICTORY OR DEATH.
>
> William Barret Travis
> Lt. Col. Comdt.
>
> P.S.
>
> The Lord is on our side. When the enemy appeared in sight we had not three bushels of corn. We have since found in deserted houses 80 to 90 bushels and got into the walls 20 or 30 head of Beeves.
>
> Travis

The letter would later be called by some the most heroic ever written by an American, but it brought no reinforcements into the Alamo.

Outside the walls, the Mexicans set up their own fortifications and artillery. Trenches were dug and soldiers occasionally fired at the Texans in the Alamo as they moved about. Both sides soon learned to keep down, especially the Mexicans for the Texans were deadly accurate. The Mexican artillery fired desolutory rounds at the fortress and occasionally the Texas cannon roared an answer, but mostly the men under Almaron Dickinson saved their powder and ammunition for better targets.

Suzanna would recall later that among the Texans were Jim Bowie, ill and hardly able to recognize even his closest acquaintance, and David Crockett, the famed Tennessee frontiersman who had come to San Antonio with several of his friends because he had heard that was the most likely place to find a fight. Crockett didn't like being penned up inside the walls and a few days after the siege began Suzanna heard him remark that he had rather go through the gates and "shoot it out with the Mexicans beyond these walls; I hate to be hemmed in." It was to Crockett that the men looked for an occasional tall tale or a tune from his fiddle to cheer them up and relieve the monotony and uncertainty of the waiting.

Other messengers went out with appeals for help and provisions, but still none came to reinforce the small band. Each day the Mexican earthworks crept a little closer and each day, the men inside the fort looked in vain toward the east, the direction from which help must come. Suzanna and the child Angelina, along with the other women and children were assigned to small rooms in the Alamo Chapel where they would be comparatively safe from the Mexican bullets.

Finally on March 1, after the fortress had been besieged for eight days, a small contingent of men arrived from Gonzales. There were thirty-two of them, including several whom Suzanna and her husband had known back in the little town where the revolution had begun — where the first shot had been fired by a cannon manned by Almaron Dickinson and some of his friends. The thirty-two had come as a result of Travis' message sent out on the first day of the siege by couriers Smith and Sutherland. They were determined that the record the Gonzales men had established the previous October would not be eclipsed by their failure to heed Travis' call for help.

There was much rejoicing by Suzanna and Almaron at the arrival of these friends and much to talk about. News of home and neighbors was a welcome change for them and although the number of reinforcements was smaller than needed, it was hoped that they were only the first of many who would heed Travis' plea for assistance.

Meanwhile at Washington-on-the-Brazos the delegates to a convention called by the General Council of the provisional government of Texas the previous December, were beginning their deliberations regarding the future of Texas. Among those in attendance were Jesse B. Badgett and Samuel A. Maverick who were elected by the men in the Alamo on February 1. Although they would never learn of it inside the besieged fortress, the Texans at Washington-on-the-Brazos would declare Texas independent of Mexico, write a constitution, and set up an *ad interim* government for the new republic. The declaration of independence was signed on March 2 while the Alamo garrison waited for reinforcements and watched the Mexican trenchworks draw an ever-tightening circle around the fortress.

On March 3, James Bonham, whom Travis had sent with an appeal for help to Colonel James Fannin at Goliad, returned with the message that no help would be coming from that quarter. The Mexicans were now so close to the outer walls that Bonham had had to brave a hail of bullets as he raced past the lines and through the gates of the fortress.

That same night, the last messenger from the Alamo to the outside world was sent out in a desperate appeal for help. John W. Smith, one of the scouts who first spotted the Mexican Army beyond San Antonio was Travis' choice to carry the message — this one to the president of the convention at Washington-on-the-Brazos. Some of the other men also wrote letters and Travis sent along personal letters to his friend Jesse Grimes, one of the delegates attending the convention, and to David Ayers, with whom Travis had left his young son, Charles. To Grimes he wrote:

> Let the Convention go and make a declaration of independence, and we will then understand, and the world will understand, what we are fighting for. If independence is not declared, I shall lay down my arms, and so will the men under my command. But under the flag of independence, we are ready to peril our lives a hundred times a day. . . .

To Ayers Travis wrote:

> Take care of my little boy. If the country should be saved, I may make him a splendid fortune; but if the country should be lost and I should perish, he will have nothing but the proud recollection that he is the son of a man who died for his country.

Unknown to Travis and his men in the Alamo, the convention had the day before adopted a declaration of independence and if they had some way to learn of the important event, could have raised "the flag of independence" over the walls of the besieged fortress.

When the messages were finished, the last which would leave the Alamo, Travis handed them to Smith and the scout rode with them into the night.

The next morning, March 4, the Mexican fortifications ringing the Alamo seemed closer than ever. A new battery of artillery had been set up north of the fortress and its fire was doing a lot of damage both to the north wall and to the morale of the Texans in the enclosure. To make matters worse, some of the Mexicans who had entered the Alamo with the Texans began to slip away at night and rejoin their relatives in town or in Santa Anna's army. One of these in particular had an interesting story to relate to the Mexican general. According to her story the Texans were few in number; they were short on ammunition and supplies, and she believed the fort could be easily taken. Suzanna would forever after believe that the woman was Mrs. Horace Alsbury, a daughter of the only one of the Navarro family who refused to join the Texans in their fight against Santa Anna. Long after the revolution, Suzanna would refuse to ever be in the same house with Mrs. Alsbury.

The night of the fourth of March and on into that of the fifth, the Mexicans drew closer and still no help came. Late in the evening of the fifth, as Suzanna watched from a nearby building, Travis called all his men together in the courtyard and told them of his fears that no help was coming, but that he was determined to stay and fight. Only three choices were available to them — surrender, try to escape or stay and fight alongside him. He urged them to stay, but left the choice up to each individual. Those who didn't want to stay should let it be known.

Only one man chose to try an escape. Moses Rose, a veteran of Napoleon's army and the Napoleonic Wars, let it be known that he would prefer not to stay and in a little while he had scaled the wall and was gone.

The night passed slowly for the men in the Alamo, but the Mexican soldiers were busy all night. The time had come to storm the fortress and the troops were getting into position for the assault which Santa Anna had scheduled for five o'clock in the morning.

The men inside the Alamo were busy too. Travis was everywhere, seeing to the rebuilding of the battered wall. He took time out from these chores to pay a visit to the chapel where Suzanna and Angelina, along with the other women and children, waited. Always fond of children, Travis was especially intrigued with little Angelina. Almost as if on impulse, he removed from his finger a gold ring with a black stone, put it on a piece of string and looped it about the child's neck. The act had taken only a brief moment and just as quickly he was gone — back to the task of reinforcing the walls.

At last, the Texans lay down for a brief rest — a rest that would be interrupted in a few hours by a Mexican bugler sounding the attack.

In her small room Suzanna could see nothing of the fighting, but she could hear the sounds of battle as the Mexicans surged against the walls, fell back, and came on again. Her first glimpse of what was happening outside her room came when a 16-year-old youth from Gonzales, Galba Fuqua, stumbled through the door to tell her something. He had been shot through both jaws and talking was difficult. Twice he tried to deliver the message, holding his jaws together with his hands on the last try. Failing to speak, he rushed through the door and back into the fight raging outside.

Soon Suzanna knew that the Mexicans were inside the fortress for Almaron, taking a moment from his duties with the artillery, rushed into the room saying "Great God, Sue, the Mexicans are inside our walls!" Clutching his wife and child to him for a moment, he admonished Suzanna, "If they spare you, save my child." Then he was gone and that was the last time she saw him. As the noise outside grew louder she knew the end was near. Calmly she waited, little Angelina clutched close beside her.

Suddenly, Jacob Walker, one of the cannoneers burst through the doorway followed by several Mexican soldiers. Ignoring Suzanna and the other women and children in the room, the soldiers calmly shot him and hoisted his body up on their bayonets "like a bundle of hay."

Soon it was all over and the sound of gunfire died away. Suzanna and Angelina were ordered from their room and placed in another small enclosure near the main entrance. Here were brought the other women and children to await Santa Anna's decision on what to do with them.

A Mexican officer appeared and asked in English "Is Mrs. Dickinson here?" At first she was afraid to answer, but when the question was repeated, Suzanna stepped forward. The officer ordered her to follow him if she wished to save her life. Once outside, she could see the still forms of the Texans lying about the enclosure. The body of David Crockett, his coonskin cap nearby, lay between the church and the long barracks. The horrible scene which greeted her as she followed the officer across the courtyard was more than she could comprehend. She would remember almost nothing of it. Even the stray bullet which struck her in the leg as she crossed to the main gate seemed only a minor annoyance although she had to be helped to walk.

The women and children were taken into town, there to await on audience with Santa Anna. Suzanna and Angelina found themselves back in the big house on Main Plaza where Mrs. Musquiz and other members of the Musquiz family awaited them.

The few survivors, all women and children, after spending a restless night wondering what their fate was to be, were finally brought before Santa Anna on March 7. When it was Suzanna's turn, she was surprised at the Mexican general's concern. His treatment seemed kind and this she credited to Mrs. Musquiz who she had learned had pleaded with Santa Anna to spare the women and children. The general had listened to the entreaty and finally had agreed that no women or children would be harmed. But Suzanna's relief at being treated kindly was short-lived for Santa Anna took a particular interest in little Angelina. He pointed out through his interpreter that the child was now without a father and that he would send both Angelina and her mother to Mexico where they would both be cared for. Suzanna rebelled at the thought and finally General Almonte, Santa Anna's aide, came to her rescue and persuaded Santa Anna to give up the idea.

Instead, Suzanna and Angelina would be sent as messengers to Gonzales to let the Texans know that Santa Anna was determined to put down all resistance. So on the morning of March 11, Suzanna, escorted by Almonte's servant Ben, was mounted on a horse and sent to Gonzales with the admonition that she tell the Texans that they could expect the same fate as that which had befallen the Alamo victims unless they laid down their arms and ceased their resistance to the Mexican government.

As she rode along, little Angelina held close beside her, Suzanna could not help but reflect upon all that had befallen her during the past two weeks and more. Happily she had gone to San Antonio with Almaron who believed so strongly in the fight the Texans were waging against the Mexican dictator. Now her husband and more than 180 others had been slain and Santa Anna had chosen her to bear the message of the fall of the Alamo to all of Texas. During the past few days she had seen the smoke rising from the fires upon which the bodies of the Texans had been burned and the smell of burning flesh lingered yet in her nostrils. Strange that she should be spared and stranger still that she should be chosen to tell the others of what she had witnessed in an effort to persuade them to cease their resistance.

Shortly after the little party crossed the Salado east of San Antonio, they stumbled across another survivor of the terrible slaughter. It was Joe, the faithful slave who had belonged to Colonel Travis. He too had been brought before Santa Anna after the battle and told that he would soon be a free man. The Mexican general even paraded the troops for Joe in an attempt to impress upon Travis' servant the size of the force which the Texans must face. Joe had slipped away from San Antonio and was also on his way to Gonzales. He would be good company to have on the long journey.

Finally after travelling all day on the 11th and 12th and until noon on the 13th, the little party was met by three scouts led by the famous frontiersman "Deaf" Smith. Sam Houston, now the commander-in-chief of the Texan Army had sent them out from Gonzales to learn, if possible, why the Alamo signal cannon had been silent for the last few days. The news Suzanna related was not unexpected and when she had poured out the story to the scouts, Henry Karnes raced with the news to Houston's camp, leaving the other scouts to escort the pitiful little group the remaining distance to Gonzales.

Arriving at the Texans' camp, Suzanna again repeated the story of the Alamo's fall, this time to Houston himself who wept like a child as he listened. Turning to his men, Houston ordered an immediate retreat in an attempt to draw Santa Anna farther and farther into Texas where he might be defeated. Though she may not have realized it at the time, Suzanna Dickinson had brought to the Texans a battle cry and a cause around which they could rally. At the battle of San Jacinto a little more than a month later they would avenge the massacre of their fellow soldiers and "Remember the Alamo" would echo across the field of battle upon which the independence of Texas was finally won.

Suzanna Dickinson lived for more than half a century after her harrowing experience at the Alamo in 1836. She became known as the

"Lady of the Alamo" and little Angelina was known as the "Babe of the Alamo." Suzanna's account of the last days of the little garrison was one of only a few such accounts available and she was often called upon to repeat it. She became a citizen of the new Republic of Texas, and later the State of Texas, making her home for a time in Houston where she remarried in 1838. Her second husband, Francis P. Herring, died a few years after their marriage and Suzanna was forced to take in washing to support herself and Angelina. For a time she also operated a boarding house. In 1847, she was married to Peter Bellis who built for her a house on a lot which the couple purchased in Houston. Unfortunately the marriage did not last and Bellis and Suzanna were divorced a few years later.

In 1849, Suzanna was discovered by Dr. Rufus C. Burleson, pastor of the First Baptist Church of Houston, living almost in poverty in that city. She attended a revival meeting being conducted by Dr. Burleson and later was baptised by him and became a member of his church. Burleson wrote of the great crowd of people "who crowded the Banks of Buffalo Bayou one Sabbath evening to see her baptised. During all my pastorate in Houston, and especially during the cholera epidemic, she was a zealous co-laborer of mine in every good work."

During all these years, the child Angelina was growing into young womanhood and in 1851, she married John M. Griffith of Houston. The marriage ceremony was performed by Dr. Burleson in the First Baptist Church of Houston. The couple lived near Angelina's mother for a time, then moved to Montgomery County to live on a farm. In 1855, the Legislature granted to Angelina the bounty and donation land due her father as a soldier in the army of the Republic of Texas. Located in Clay County, the land consisted of more than two thousand-five hundred acres.

As for Suzanna, she soon met and married John W. Hannig, a man sixteen years her junior, who became a wealthy Austin merchant. Moving to Austin, the couple lived happily and comfortably in a home in north Austin where Suzanna often received guests who wished to hear from her lips the story of the last days of the Alamo. Although she was extremely reluctant to talk about her role in the incident, she was often called upon to vouch for the presence in the fortress of some of the victims of the massacre as their heirs applied for the land due them.

It was not until 1881 that she paid a return visit to the Alamo. On that occasion she was accompanied by a reporter for the San Antonio *Express* who wrote:

> She can give but little of the struggle, as she was in a little dark room in the rear of the building. The party yesterday entered this appartment, and even with a candle could scarcely see each other's faces. The old lady recognized almost every stone, however, and the

arch overhead and the corners she said, with tears in her eyes, came back as vividly to memory as though her experiences of yore had been but yesterday. She showed the reporter where her couch had stood, and the window through which she peeped to see the blood of noble men seeping into the ground, and the bodies of heroes lying cold in death . . . They were all bloody, and crimson springs coursed the yard. The old lady says she doesn't know how it all happened, yet tells a great deal. What became of her husband, Al Marion Dickinson, she cannot tell, but saw him last when he went from her presence with gun in hand to die for his country . . . At the time of the fatal encounter, all were ready for the fray, and all prepared to die for the nationality of the republic of Texas. True womanly courage is exemplified by the conduct of Mrs. Hannig. She loved her own, and that was the child she hugged to her bosom. Her life had been endangered, and they wanted to take her child away from her, but she would not concede, and so she subjected herself to trials, looking consequences squarely in the face, and knowing that firearms would be bound to bring about her ultimate vindication.

Suzanna Dickinson Hannig died on October 7, 1883, and was buried in Oakwood Cemetery in Austin. Her husband, John W. Hannig, who died only seven years later, erected a simple stone at her gravesite with the inscription:

We only know that thou hast gone
And that the same relentless tide
Which bore thee from us still glides
And we who mourn thee with it glide.

# Cynthia Ann Parker

CYNTHIA ANN PARKER

# Cynthia Ann Parker

by
RUPERT N. RICHARDSON

The story of Cynthia Ann Parker is etched deep in the history and saga of the Southwest. A child of the frontier, she was made an Indian captive at the age of nine and after twenty-five years with the Comanches she was torn away from her Indian people and made a captive of the forgotten people of her childhood. Her life is an epitome of frontier grief and tragedy.

At Parker's Fort in Central Texas, between the present towns of Mexia and Groesbeck, the morning of May 19, 1836 dawned with the promise of clear weather, good for farming. Everybody was busy, for the Parker clan and their associates had recently returned from the Runaway Scrape. Along with thousands of other Texans they had fled eastward at the news of the coming of the Mexican armies. The flooding Trinity had delayed them. And, tortured with fear while they were waiting for a ferry, they heard the glorious news of Sam Houston's victory at San Jacinto and also Houston's admonition that they go back home. After a short delay they returned to their stockade and took up the routine of life that had been broken a few weeks before.

Parker's Fort was a good pioneer defense complex. A rectangular enclosure, 171 by 242 feet of log pickets twelve feet high, sharpened at the top, enclosed cabins for families. Two block houses at diagonal corners served as bastions from which riflemen might defend all four sides. But now that the terror of the Mexican invasion was behind them the pioneers relaxed and let down their guard. Almost three years residence there with little molestation had dulled their sense of alertness and caution. A company of rangers commanded by one of the Parkers since the preceding October had been disbanded a few days before. James W. Parker, who in his *Narrative* states that he was commander of the fort, and three other men left unarmed that morning for a farm a mile away. Several other men were working in fields in the vicinity. Some were residents of the fort; others were residing in their own cabins at or near their fields. Elder John Parker, seventy-nine, patriarch of the family, and five other men able to bear arms were left there, more by ordinary circumstances it seems than through any fear of an attack on the place. From the slender records, it appears that even their arms were not in readiness.

"At the cry of Indians all was in a state of confusion," wrote Mrs. Rachel

Plummer, daughter of James W. Parker, whose *Narrative* was written some three years later, after her return from Indian captivity. Still hers is the best eye-witness account of what took place at the fort on that day of tragedies. Other sources vary in respect to details.

Estimates of the number of Indians range from 300 to 700. They were principally Comanches, with possibly a few Kiowas, and certainly there were some Kichais. The last named were Indians of the vicinity. After the alarm and while the Indians were a considerable distance away, the women and children began to flee toward the Navasota River ("Navisott") bottom a short distance away, where they hid in the brush. One man with his family joined them in the flight.

Meanwhile two Indians came up to the fort, bearing a white flag. Benjamin Parker, the bachelor son of Elder John, went out to treat with them. They indicated that they were friendly and had come for a beef and for directions to a good camping place. Benjamin Parker went back into the fort and reported that, for all their pretense at friendliness, he believed the visitors were hostile, actually on the warpath.

The young man evidently deemed himself expendable, for over the protest of his brother, Silas, he returned to the Indians, who had moved closer in. It is evident that he hoped to parlay awhile and give his companions a little more time to prepare for defense. His heroic course did not buy much time, however. The red men set upon him with their spears at once, rushed upon the fort and took it over, and proceeded with their plunder, rapine, and murder. Confused and without organization, the defenders did not have time to close the gates or to concentrate their strength in one of the block houses, where they might have held out for a while at least. Most of the women and children had escaped before the marauders rushed in.

Mrs. Rachel Plummer had not fled with the other women and children. Her little son, James Pratt, was too young to run and too heavy to carry. When she did try to escape, the Indians overtook her, knocked her unconscious with a hoe, drug her by the hair for some distance, and took her and her little boy away into captivity. They also took captive her aunt, Mrs. Elizabeth Kellogg. Elder John Parker and wife also fled too late. The marauders overtook, killed and scalped the old patriarch. His wife was stabbed, raped, and left for dead, but was rescued by a party after the marauders left.

Other heroism must be credited to the white people. Mrs. Sarah Nixon had hurried with the news to the men in the fields and some of them rushed into the affair where the odds were against them one hundred to one. David Faulkenberry seized his rifle from his cabin and ran toward the fort. He came upon Mrs. Lucy Parker, wife of Silas Parker who had just died fighting, and their two younger children. Indian horsemen had already ridden away with Cynthia Ann and John, the Silas Parkers' daughter and son, age nine and six respectively, and were forcing Mrs. Parker and the two little children to follow. Displaying his rifle, threatening to fire every moment but never firing and thus disarming himself, Faulkenberry escorted the woman and children toward a belt of timber as mounted Indians followed, threatening to kill the defender and regain the captives. But the marauders would hold off each time as the intrepid frontiersman aimed his rifle at the leader, finger on the trigger. In this scene Mrs. Parker's unnamed dog earned a hero's medal. As his mistress and her children with their protector were about to enter the woods and thereby escape from the pursuing horsemen, one Indian made a reckless charge and got so near that the dog seized his horse by the nose, and horse and rider somersaulted into a ravine. At this moment other armed men arrived to aid Faulkenberry and the group of Indians retreated. Besides David Faulkenberry, whose courage and coolness rescued Mrs. Silas Parker and her two younger children, Evan Faulkenberry, Silas Bates, and Abram Anglin, members of the fort party or neighbors, helped in the rescue.

A summation of the bloody episode is: five killed — Elder John Parker and his two sons Benjamin and Silas; Samuel Frost and his young son, Robert. Mrs. John Parker ("Granny") was seriously wounded. Five persons were taken captive — Cynthia Ann and John Parker, children of the slain Silas Parker and Mrs. Silas Parker; Mrs. Elizabeth Kellogg, sister-in-law of the Parker brothers; and Mrs. Rachel Plummer, daughter of James W. Parker, and her little son, James Pratt Plummer. Some twenty persons escaped from the fort without serious injury, and it appears that the men who came to the aid of those in the fort escaped without casualty.

At twilight, Abram Anglin and Evan Faulkenberry returned to the fort to aid any persons who might have survived. On their way, at Seth Anglin's cabin, they rescued Mrs. John Parker ("Granny") who had been severely wounded, but had managed to walk and crawl to the cabin, three-quarters of a mile away. There were no other survivors. On the following morning a party of three returned, managed to find a little food that had not been destroyed or taken away, and found five or six horses. Fearing that the Indians might be lurking in the vicinity, they did not take time to bury the dead. They did not succeed in contacting the larger party that had fled from the fort the preceding day and were now hidden in the brush in charge of James W. Parker who had joined them. With horses and food the smaller party of four or five persons made its way without difficulty to Fort Houston, at the site of Palestine, some sixty miles away. The larger group, consisting of James W. Parker, F.E. Dwight, and some nineteen women and children found ahead of them a trail of hunger, thorns, tears and blood. After six days they reached Tinnin's, where the old San Antonio-

Nacogdoches road crossed the Navasota River. Learning of their approach, two generous hearted men, Carter and Courting, went out to meet them with five horses, and the people of that frontier settlement shared their slender stock of food and clothing. Thirty days later a band of twelve men from Fort Houston returned to Parker's Fort and buried the bones of those slain. They found the buildings still standing, but crops had been destroyed, horses had been stolen, nearly all the cattle killed, and nothing that would break was left unbroken. Soon most of the Fort Parker group returned to the place and renewed their habitation there.

This branch of the early-day Parker family of Texas was a sturdy set of folks, a number of whom attained renown. Eight have been given sketches in the *Handbook of Texas*. The progenitor was Elder John. He was a veteran of the American Revolution. Born in Virginia in 1757, he moved to Elbert County, Georgia, thence to Bedford County, Tennessee, in 1802, and to Illinois in 1818. With his wife, Sally (White) Parker, "Granny", and three or more of his sons and their families he came to Texas in 1833 and settled that year on the Navasota River, near the site of Groesbeck. Elder John Parker's son, Nathaniel, who never moved to Texas, was a member of the senate of Illinois for some years. Parker's Fort was built a year after the arrival of the party. John Parker was a preacher, or elder, of the Primitive Baptist Church.

The family had a pronounced bent toward the ministry. Elder Daniel Parker (1781-1844), oldest son of Elder John and Sallie Parker, is noted for having organized a church of some thirty-six members in Illinois and moving with the body to Texas, where the church was established and continued. He had served in the senate of Illinois and was elected to the Texas Congress in 1839, but he could not be seated because of constitutional limitations on the ministry. Daniel Parker's son, Benjamin F. (1819-1896), bearing the same name as that of his uncle who was slain at Parker's Fort, was a minister and Texas legislator. Isaac Parker (1793-1883), son of Elder John, fought in the Texas Revolution, served in the Texas Congress, in the Texas Constitutional Convention of 1845, and in the Texas legislature. Isaac's brother, Silas, who, it will be recalled, fell bravely defending Parker's Fort, had by authority of the general council of Texas in 1835-1836 employed and led a company of rangers to protect the frontier.

The next generation of Parkers also attained renown. Cynthia Ann and John Parker, children of Silas and Lucy (Duty) Parker were taken away Indian captives, and Quanah, son of Cynthia Ann, was the last distinguished Comanche chief.

Now the family story centers on James W. Parker (1797-1865), son of Elder John Parker. In his *Narrative of Perilous Adventures*, published in 1844, James W. Parker precedes his name with "Reverend." It must be said, however, that with the time and energy he devoted to other affairs he surely had but little time for the ministry. He stated in his *Narrative* that he hoped to realize from its sale funds to enable him to secure the release from the Indians of his niece, Cynthia Ann, daughter of his brother Silas who was slain at Parker's Fort in 1836. He was a member of the Consultation, the provisional government that met in the fall of 1835 and made possible the success of the Texas Revolution. He also had been a member of a ranger company during the Revolution and may have commanded it.

According to his *Narrative*, James W. Parker worked for several years in a state of desperation, which at times became recklessness, and exhausted his estate to secure the release of his captive daughter, grand child, and other kin. Some things he did must have been disturbing to men both red and white who were seeking to establish a measure of security and stability along the frontier. The death of his brother, John, near Cape Giradeau, Missouri, at the hands of Delaware Indians about 1812 had made him "hostile and bitter." At times he expressed the hope that he might "be charitable and follow the admonition of the Divine Master" in his relations with the Indians, but in practice he occasionably conformed to Walter Prescott Webb's descriptive phrase concerning certain Texas Rangers — " Indian exterminators."

Little information is extant about the course the depredators of Parker's Fort pursued after their bloody raid on that outpost. About all that is known comes from Mrs. Plummer's *Narrative*, and often she could not comprehend or was not permitted to know what was taking place. She relates that after a few days travel her Aunt Elizabeth (Mrs. Kellogg) "fell to the 'Kitchawas'" (Kichais), a small tribe of the Caddoan family living in North Central Texas. This fact is significant, for it indicates that neighboring Indians were with the aggregation of plainsmen that made the attack and likely guided their fierce allies to the stockade. It is not unlikely that the Indians of the region had been antagonized by the people of the fort or the ranger company that had operated in the vicinity from October until May, 1835-1836. Mrs. Plummer also relates that her niece and nephew, Cynthia Ann and John Parker, "fell to another portion of the Comanches," that is, to another Comanche tribe or division.

As the Indians and captives moved northward, James Pratt, Mrs. Plummer's little son not more than two, was taken away from her and she never saw him again. She was taken on northward, crossing the Red River and the upper Arkansas, into a country where mountain peaks were covered with eternal snow, to a locality evidently far north of Santa Fe, New Mexico. Indeed, it has been suggested that she was too far north for the range of the Yamparikas, the northernmost of Comanche divisions, and that she must have been traded to the Shoshonis, Yutes, or other mountain Indians. She suffered indescribable cruelty at the hands of the natives. They seized, tortured, and killed in her presence an infant born to her in captivity. She was better treated after she fought and almost killed an Indian woman, whose "slave" she was. Mexican traders bought her of her captors and took her to Santa Fe, a journey southward that took seventeen days. There, through the generosity of Colonel and Mrs. William Donahue, American traders in Santa Fe, she was purchased, escorted to Independence, Missouri, and thence to the home of her father, James W. Parker, then residing in Montgomery County, Southeast Texas. She arrived at her father's home on February 19, 1838. Exposure, ill treatment, and grief had ruined her health. She lived only about a year thereafter.

According to the written record that he left, James W. Parker worked around the calendar for the release of the captives. In July 1836, he appealed to General Sam Houston, then sojourning in East Texas near San Augustine trying to heal the ankle that had been shattered at San Jacinto. Parker wanted to raise a company of men to protect the frontier and chastise the Indians. Houston was not sympathetic with the idea of a military company. He thought a treaty with the Indians would be better than war. Again, with the aid of other influential frontiersmen, Parker went to Nacogdoches and appealed to General Houston, but again his request was denied. At Nacogdoches he was rejoiced to see his sister-in-law, Mrs. Elizabeth Kellogg, whom Delaware Indian traders had bought and brought in. Houston paid the Delawares $150 for their services. On their way home, Parker shot and killed an Indian whom Mrs. Kellogg had identified as one of the marauders at Parker's Fort.

In his efforts to recover the other prisoners, James W. Parker journeyed over much of North Texas and present-day Oklahoma, seeking to exploit such sources as Holland Coffee's Indian traders along the Red River. Again, in 1837, he appealed to Sam Houston, now President; and according to his *Narrative* he was proceeding to raise a volunteer military company by Houston's authority, when the order came from the President to discontinue recruiting and disband the force. Obviously Houston feared that, with a company at his command, the bellicose parson would raise more fury than he would quiet.

Through perils and privations Parker went on with the search for the Indian captives, but his efforts availed nothing. It has been related already that his daughter, Mrs. Rachel Plummer, was returned to him in February, 1838, but her rescue was in no way related to Parker's efforts. His journey and labors continued for the release of his grandson, James Pratt Plummer, and his niece and nephew, Cynthia Ann and John, daughter and son of his brother, Silas, who had died in defense of Parker's Fort. In his *Narrative* he states that at Fort Gibson, Indian Territory, on January 15, 1843, he found his grandson, James Pratt Plummer, and his nephew John Parker, who had been purchased by Indian traders. He recognized his grandson by his resemblance to his daughter, the boy's mother. He was grieved when his grandson refused to have anything to do with him but ran away and sought to hide in a dragoon camp nearby. Finally he succeeded in making the child understand his relationship to him, that he was his mother's father but that his mother was dead. He explained to the boy that his father was living. Parker adds that they reached home safely, that his grandson soon learned to speak English; and, writing of both boys adds that "they are now [1844, at the time of the writing of his journal] doing well." Still, a joint resolution of the Texas Congress, approved June 27, 1845 authorized the treasurer to pay to Honorable Isaac Parker $300 to be applied in securing the release of John Parker, said to be a prisoner with the Keechi tribe. So it seems that not all the Parker family recognized as John Parker the lad whom James W. Parker had brought home with his grandson.

That John Parker was returned to his mother and grew to manhood with her is indicated, however, by Captain R.B. Marcy's *Report of the Exploration of the Red River of Louisiana*, 1852, page 103, which states that the "brother of the white woman named Parker, captured with her and later restored to his people" had talked with him, telling him that he had visited with the Comanches at the behest of his mother and sought unsuccessfully to persuade his sister to return to her people. Still, a story about John Parker that appeared in print as early as 1879 in a *Pictoral History* of Texas, by the Reverend Homer S. Thrall may not be good history, but it is much more romantic that the version sustained by the records.

This story, which Thrall does not verify, appears in numberless books published later. It is that John was not restored to his people but grew to manhood with the red men, became a Comanche in every respect except the color of his hair, eyes, and skin. John, according to the story, accompanied a raiding party into Mexico and on the expedition fell in love with Doña Juanita, a fair young Mexican captive. As the party returned northward toward the Comanche range in Texas, John was prostrated with smallpox. The raiding band moved on but permitted Doña Juanita to stay with John and care for him. John recovered, they were married, and "settled on a stock ranch in the far West." When the Civil War broke out John joined a Mexican company in the Confederate service and was noted for his gallantry and daring. He refused, however, to leave the soil of Texas for that of Louisiana. According to James De Shields, in his *Border Wars of Texas*, the couple was living on a ranch in Mexico at about 1885.

Information about Cynthia Ann Parker during her life of more than two decades with the Indians is exceedingly meager. From time to time Indian traders and Indian agents heard of her: but they found it difficult to contact her and for two reasons made no progress toward recovering her from the Indians, because she did not want to leave the Indians and because the Indians would not consider parting with her.

It is recorded in the federal archives that in 1846 Colonel Leonard Williams, acting as agent for the United States, offered goods for her worth several hundred dollars; but she was claimed by a chief who refused to give her up. Furthermore, when the white men sought to confer with her she would run away and hide. Robert S. Neighbors, special Indian agent, reported in 1847 that she was held by the Tenawish (Tenawa) Comanches who ranged along the upper Red River. In the years immediately following, the agent sought to cultivate these middle Comanches, but he never contacted Cynthia Ann. He reported that the chiefs kept promising to give her up but never did so. Some chiefs with whom he talked thought it would take force to release her. Neighbors added that "it might be an act of humanity if the [Indian] Department set her free." It never occurred to the white men that taking her away from the Indians would simply make her a captive again. Captain R.B. Marcy's report made in 1852 has been referred to in preceding pages and may well be quoted in full:

> There is at this time a white woman among the Middle Comanches, by the name of Parker, who, with her brother, was captured while they were young children, from their house in the western part of Texas. This woman has adopted all the habits and peculiarities of the Comanches; has an Indian husband and children, and cannot be persuaded to leave them. The brother of the woman, who had been ransomed by a trader and brought home to his relatives, was sent by his mother for the purpose of endeavoring to prevail upon his sister to leave the Indians and return to the family; but he stated to me that on his arrival she refused to listen to the proposition, saying that her husband, children, and all that she held most dear were with the Indians and there she would remain.

It appears that Cynthia Ann was with the Nokoni (wanderers) or Detsanayuka (bad campers — people who never take the trouble to fix up good camps since they never stay long in the same place). They were never brought into treaty relationship with Texas or the United States before the Civil War. These Comanches were associated with and they may have merged into a larger Comanche division ranging principally in the High Plains, the Kwahadis (antelopes). Another explanation of the origin of the Kwahadi name is Qua-he-hu-ke, meaning back-shade, so called because in their treeless country the only way to shade the face was to turn one's back to the sun. Cynthia Ann Parker was the wife of Chief Peta Nacona. Chief Baldwin

Parker, grandson of Peta Nacona and Cynthia Ann, stated to the writer that his grandfather, of the Nokoni Comanches, joined the Kwahadis and was recognized as a chief.

The capture of Cynthia Ann by white men was an accident, an episode in a relentless campaign of state and federal troops and armed citizens against the Indians of Northwest Texas. Before the story of her re-capture is told it seems pertinent to give a summary of the North Texas frontier situation in the middle decades of the Nineteenth Century. During the quarter century between the Texas Revolution and the Civil War, Texans relentlessly appropriated the country of the Indians. Indeed, neither as a republic nor as a state did the commonwealth ever recognize that the red men had any possessory right to the land. After annexation in 1845 the state looked to the general government to protect the frontier people against Indian maraudings. This was an exceedingly difficult task, for the public lands, the most important factor in the control of Indians, belonged to the state. Settlers appropriated millions of acres annually, the Indians resisted, and wars were inevitable.

Most Indian tribes, the Comanches and Kiowas especially, made the raiding of the settlements a way of life. They harried the people of the North Mexican states, took away thousands of horses and hundreds of captives, and from time to time turned their raids against the Texas frontier. A cordon of military posts extending in an irregular line from Fort Belknap near the site of Graham in North Texas to Fort Clark near the Rio Grande was established in 1851-1852, but the forts helped only a little.

On land supplied by the state, the federal government established Indian reservations in 1855: a small home of four square leagues for the Comanches on the Clear Fork of the Brazos in present Throckmorton County and another of eight leagues on the Brazos in present Young County for the lesser sedentary tribes. On both reservations the Indians made encouraging progress, but only three or four hundred Comanches came to their reservation and remained. Maraudings continued, the reservation Indians were blamed, unjustly so it appears, and the hostility of the frontier white people toward the red people became so great that the Indian administration was obliged to remove the Indians to the Indian Territory in 1859.

Meanwhile depredations by wild Indians continued and did not diminish after the removal of the reservation people. In retaliation against incursions from north of the Red River, state and federal troops, joined by friendly Indians from the Brazos Reservation until the time of removal, made repeated campaigns against Indians that extended far beyond the borders of Texas. In April, 1858 Captain John S. Ford, with 102 rangers and a select force of Brazos Reservation Indians under the command of their agent, Shapley P. Ross, attacked a Comanche village on Little Robe Creek, north of the South Canadian River in present Oklahoma and left seventy-six dead Indians at the place. In September following, Earl Van Dorn of the famed Second United States Cavalry, with four companies of troopers and a hundred Indians under Lawrence Sullivan Ross, son of the Brazos Indian agent and destined to become governor of Texas, attacked a Comanche camp near present Rush Springs, Oklahoma and killed fifty-six warriors. The losses were not all on the side of the Indians. Van Dorn, Ross, and several of their men were severely wounded, and Lieutenant Cornelius Van Camp, one sergeant, and three privates lay dead.

There were other campaigns against Indians, other Indian and troop losses, but the marauding continued. From the Red River to the San Saba, Indians stole horses, burned buildings and tortured and killed captives. They did not confine their assaults to the new settlements but struck deep into counties where the settlers had come to have a sense of security, such as Parker, Erath, and Bosque in Central Texas.

In November, 1860, a band of some sixty Comanche warriors left a bloody trail through Jack, Parker, and Palo Pinto Counties. In Jack County they killed five or six people, among them John Brown, who was out racing to warn neighbors of their approach. Brown entered a thicket and resisted to the end, but he had no other weapon than a pocket knife. The pillagers wounded, mutilated, or otherwise assaulted eight or ten other people, besides plundering homes, killing and stealing stock. They were utterly unpredictable. They might hold part of a family captive and tell the other to "*vamoos*." (Most Comanches spoke a little Spanish.) Then they might overtake those who were fleeing and torture or kill them. They might set fire to a house or be satisfied just to loot it, slitting open feather beds and pillows and smashing everything that would break. Frequently they wounded or killed their victims with clubs and rocks, saving their arrows and bullets for more formidable foes. They attacked the Ezra Sherman family, who lived on Skaggs Prairie, Palo Pinto County, stabbed, raped and left for dead Mrs. Sherman and drove the rest of the family away. Mrs. Sherman died shortly thereafter. Along with various other items they carried away her Bible, for paper made excellent stuffing for shields.

News of such macabre carryings on spread with the speed of fast horses and created terror and a measure of panic in all Northwest Texas of that day. Men from Palo Pinto and adjoining counties gathered, elected J.H. Cureton, a seasoned frontiersman, captain and prepared for a campaign. Meanwhile, pursuant to the orders of Governor Sam Houston, Lawrence S. Ross had enlisted a company of state rangers in the Waco country and proceeded to the vicinity of Fort Belknap. Cureton and Ross united their forces and to their strength was added twenty troopers from the Second United States Cavalry at Camp Cooper under Sergeant W. Spangler. The citizens company,

Ross's forces, and the cavalry aggregated some hundred and thirty men.

Ross set out in a northwesterly direction and evidently had little trouble following the trail of marauding Indians from the Rolling Plains country to the settlements. It is reported, furthermore that he had received information of a Comanche encampment on the Pease River. With his company and the cavalry — the citizens company had been delayed a few hours — he came upon a band of Comanches on Mule Creek, a small tributary of the Pease River near present Margaret, Texas on December 19, 1860.

Lines of sand hills that run parallel with the creek and a prevailing sand storm enabled the troops to take the Indians completely by surprise. The camp was made up largely of women, children, and captives engaged in processing and loading on horses and mules the carcasses of buffaloes that had been killed recently. At Ross's order the twenty cavalry troops, screened from view of the Indians by the range of hills, ran ahead and cut off the retreat of the Indians while Ross charged with forty men. A few braves tried to make a stand against the attackers, but soon all either were in flight or killed.

The white men could not distinguish the Indian women from the men, wrapped as they were in buffalo robes. In the chase Captain Ross raced two Indians riding double. The one behind, who proved to be a woman, fell from her horse mortally wounded, pulling off the front rider as she fell. The dismounted man started a stream of arrows, one of which struck Ross's horse, making the animal unmanageable. Nevertheless, with a random shot from his six-shooter, Ross broke the warrior's arm at the elbow and then shot him twice through the body. Whereupon the wounded man, in true Comanche fashion, deliberately walked to a small tree and holding to it sang his death chant. Ross inquired of his interpreter, a Mexican who had been a Comanche captive, who the warrior was and the interpreter said that he knew him, that he was Nacona, a noted chief. Through his interpreter Ross sought to induce the wounded man to surrender, but he scoffed at the idea. Ranger Benjamin Franklin Gholson, telling of the event many years later, quoted the warrior as saying that he would surrender when he was dead and then "to that captain up there." Then he thrust at Ross with a spear, but the weapon was not long enough to reach his antagonist. After this defiance the warrior was killed.

Captain Ross always believed that he was the victor over the Comanche chief Nacona. Evidence from Comanche sources indicates, however, that the man he killed was not the chief but was the chief's Mexican slave, often called Nacona's Joe, after the name of his master. More convincing is the statement of George Hunt, a Kiowa authority who got his information from old Comanches, that he was a Comanche chief named No-bah. He did not die like a Mexican captive; he defied the enemy to the end and did his death chant like a Comanche warrior. Peta Nacona (or Nocona), the Kwahadi Comanche chief, husband of Cynthia Ann Parker, was some thirty-five miles away at the time of the Pease River attack and his sons, Quanah and Pecos, were with him. In later years his son, Quanah Parker sought with vehemence to correct the "lie" that his father was killed at the Pease River fight on December 19, 1860. His Comanche descendants say that Peta Nacona died in 1864 of an infected wound.

From the point of view of our own day the fight of the Rangers and Cavalry with the Comanches at Pease River was an inglorious affair. It appears that several of the thirteen Indians killed were women. It may be repeated in defense of the white men that they could not distinguish women from men. Years later the veteran Charles Goodnight stated that "to the credit of the old Texas rangers, not one of them shot a squaw that day." He laid the reckless shooting to the cavalrymen. Captain Ross made captive an Indian boy about nine in order to protect him and took him home with him. In later years he offered to restore him to his people, but the boy refused to go.

Captain Ross was well pleased with his accomplishment. He wrote and by special messenger sent to the Fort Belknap correspondent of the *Dallas Herald* a message published January 2, 1861, that merits quoting in part.

> I have just returned to my camp from the expedition in co-operation with Captain Currington's [Cureton's] gallant company of citizens from Palo Pinto and other counties, and succeeded in killing 13 Comanche Indians and taking prisoners three others.
>
> In their possession I found the Bible of Mrs. Sherman [the woman who had been outraged and left for dead in Palo Pinto County], with her name on the fly leaf; and also the papers of Henry Rilly.
>
> I thrashed them out with my own company [and the twenty cavalrymen from Camp Cooper], Captain C being several miles in my rear owing to some mishap on the morning of the 19th (the day of the fight) and I met them (the citizens) two miles back, with all the trophies.

Then Ross added:

> I took one white woman prisoner, and she informed me that 35 warriors are to be present somewhere in the settlements, and my object is to notify the citizens of it, that they may be on their guard.

On an occasion during World War I this writer was talking casually with General Luther R. Hare, a veteran of Indian Wars of the Plains and of the Philippine Insurrection, who had retired and was once again in active service. He had been with the first contingent of troops that arrived at the scene of

Custer's last stand on the Little Bighorn River, in 1876. The writer referred to it as the "Custer massacre." The response was instantaneous: "That was not a massacre," the veteran said. "What would you call it then?" "It was a fight, a battle and the soldiers lost," he said. "If the soldiers had won, the Indians would have been killed. When white men and red fought on the Plains the stakes were life and death; nobody asked for and nobody gave quarter, everybody understood that."

So it was with Ross and his men. They were fighting Indians, and they did not know how weak or how strong the enemy were.

The frontier people likewise were elated. To Ross's message the Fort Belknap correspondent, writing on December 23, 1860, added

> The above will be good news for the frontier. The party that were killed (and the whole party were killed), are the ones who committed the inhuman butcheries in Jack County [and Palo Pinto County].
>
> The evidence is conclusive — clothes, papers, &-c being recovered from them, which proves beyond a doubt that they are the guilty wretches. Captain Ross and the men and officers under him, deserve, as they will receive, the thanks of the frontier.

Ross returned to the settlements after the Pease River attack. The citizen company stayed out a few days longer but they soon returned without any epic experience to report. The veteran Indian fighter must have known that he had not matched strength with an Indian force of any great importance. That he returned to the settlements so soon indicates that, for all the praise he gave his own troops and their civilian allies, he did not feel equal to the exactions of a long campaign against Comanches in force. Furthermore, he had wreaked vengeance for the Indian outrages and brought a measure of satisfaction to the frontier people. Another fact must be kept in mind also: these were times of tension and terror in Texas. The Secessionists were pressing their cause; an issue far greater even than frontier protection was absorbing the attention of the people. Texas was in the throes of the contest over disunion.

Lieutenant Tom Kelliheir, who had been at Ross's side for awhile in pursuit of Indians in the Pease River attack was greatly dissatisfied with himself after the contest had ended. When Ross rode up he exclaimed: "Captain, I ran me horse most to death and captured a damn squaw." He might have added too that the squaw held a baby in her arms. Soon it was discovered that the woman had light hair and blue eyes. She was greatly excited and wept pitiably. Her captors, through interpretors, sought to allay her fears, assuring her that she would not be harmed. She was, however, greatly disturbed and greatly grieved and expressed concern about her two sons. She grew morose and would not talk. Apparently she had forgotten the substantial amount of English that she must have known at the time of her capture at the age of nine and had forgotten also the experiences of her childhood, even her own name and the name of her family. Ross did, however, succeed in getting from her some important information about the Indians and the frontier.

She was taken to the ranger camp near Fort Belknap and thence to Camp Cooper, where the officers' wives looked after her and provided her and her child with clothing. Ross suspected that she might be Cynthia Ann Parker and sent for her uncle, Senator Isaac Parker, who lived at Birdville in the Fort Worth vicinity. Concerning this meeting which resulted in the positive identification of Cynthia Ann Parker, it seems well to quote the Texas historian of old, Homer S. Thrall:

> Her age and general appearance suited the object of his search, but she had lost every word of her native tongue. In a letter to us Colonel Parker says: "The moment I mentioned the name, she straightened herself in her seat, and patting herself on the breast, said, 'Cynthia Ann, Cynthia Ann.' A ray of recollection sprung up in her mind, that had been obliterated for twenty-five years. Her very countenance changed, and a pleasant smile took the place of a sullen gloom."

Her uncle took her to his home in Tarrant County. Captured in 1836 at the age of nine, Cynthia Ann Parker was now thirty-four. It is stated by James T. De Shields that shortly thereafter she was taken to Austin and conducted into the hall where the state Secession Convention was in session. She appeared to be greatly distressed, thinking that the assemblage was a meeting of war chiefs, convened to decide her fate, and she feared that the decision would be against her.

The legislature granted her a pension of $100 a year for five years and granted her a league of land. In 1862 she moved to Van Zant County and was placed in the custody of her brother, Silas M. Parker, who was charged by the law enacted that year with the support and education of her child, Topasannah (Prairie Flower).

Cynthia Ann never became reconciled to life with the people of her childhood and more than once tried, without success, to escape. Topasannah died in 1864, and her mother followed her in death that year. Cynthia Ann was buried in the Foster graveyard, Henderson County.

Cynthia Ann Parker was buried, but Texans have not let her memory die and her descendants have been very loyal in keeping alive the history and saga linked with her name.

Foremost in the perpetuation of her memory was her son, Quanah, some twelve years old when she was taken away. (Her younger son, Pecos, died in his youth.) It will be recalled that Quanah's father, Chief Peta Nacona, died when his son was about sixteen. According to Indian sources, Quanah lived for periods with the Kotostekas (Buffalo Eaters), a northern Comanche division and also with the Penatekas (Honey Eaters), the southernmost Comanches, some of whom had resided on the Comanche reservation in Texas in the 1850's. After the treaty of Medicine Lodge, 1867, all Comanches were supposed to remain on the reservation, near Fort Sill and present day Lawton, Oklahoma, but several divisions of that people continued to stay out, maintaining an independent existence and from time to time making raids on the Texas frontier settlements.

Whatever Quanah's boyhood may have been, it is certain that in young manhood he became leader of the Kwahadis, the Comanche division that refused to "swap the trial of the buffalo for that of the sheep," and fiercely resisted efforts to drive them to the reservation. They made the High Plains and adjacent canyons their home; *Comancheros* (traders from New Mexico) supplied their wants in the way of weapons, coffee, tobacco, and liquor; and they were thus able to defy the federal agents, and for a time even the troops of the United States.

At the request of Indian agent Lawrie Tatum, Colonel Ranald S. Mackenzie at Fort Richardson (Jacksboro), the greatest Indian fighter of his day, was ordered in August 1871 to force the Kwahadis to come in to the reservation. With some six hundred troops Mackenzie entered the Indian country early in October. The Kwahadis, under Quanah Parker surprised him, stampeded his stock, and caused him to lose seventy horses. Later an advance column of his force attacked the Indians near the mouth of Blanco Canyon (present Crosbyton, Texas, vicinity), but the Kwahadi warriors under Quanah fought back the soldiers until the women and children could escape. Mackenzie pursued the Indians on up the Canyon and into the High Plains on either side, but a norther, with its cold, rain, and snow forced him to give up the chase. He did not even seriously punish the Kwahadis, much less drive them to the reservation.

Some three years later Quanah led the red men in the last Indian war on the South Plains, the attack on Adobe Walls and the subsequent Red River War of 1874. This was an Indian renascence movement. A Comanche medicine man and prophet, Ísä́taí, who claimed occult powers (bullets of the enemy aimed at him fell harmlessly to the ground) set out to convince his fellow tribesmen and neighboring Indians that the "Indians were going down hill every day" and that they must take drastic steps to save their race from extermination. He pointed out that those Indians who had been longest and most closely associated with the white men were the poorest and the most miserable. The only hope for the Indian was to kill the white people and be free again.

Quanah responded to Ísataí's appeal and led a formidable force of Comanche, Cheyenne, and other Indian warriors against Adobe Walls, a buffalo hunters' stockade on the Canadian River, some sixty miles northeast of the site of Amarillo, on the morning of June 27, 1874. The attack failed, but it ended buffalo hunting in the region for the season. Now the Army poured in troops from every direction, the Indians were beaten in a series of engagements, pursued relentlessly, and driven to their reservations.

The last important Comanche band to surrender was the Kwahadi, which was escorted to the reservation in June, 1875, by Dr. J.J. Sturm, agency physician.

The intelligent Quanah now realized that the old way of life was ended and that the red men must conform to the demands of the new order. He took the name Parker, after his mother; his influence became a great stabilizing force among his people. He had a good income from leases on his lands; white friends built him a spacious house; and Quanah, Texas was named after him. In 1886 he was appointed judge of The Court of Indian Affairs. He was a member of the local school board and deputy sheriff, and Theodore Roosevelt claimed him as a friend. His children were well educated. One son, White Parker, became a Methodist preacher, noted for his eloquence; Baldwin Parker, whom this writer knew well, was unusually well informed. He used to quote his father's saying that the only thing one can have that cannot be taken away is an education. One daughter worked in a bank in Waco, Texas, and other daughters married well-to-do ranchmen.

Quanah had a deep affection for his mother, secured a daguerreotype of her and Prairie Flower and had it copied in oil. He had the remains of his mother reinterred in Post Oak Mission Cemetery near Cache, Oklahoma. This was done with funds appropriated by an act of Congress in 1910. A.C. Birdsong, Quanah Parker's son-in-law, an employee of the Indian service in Oklahoma, identified her remains and also the remains of Prairie Flower which were reinterred as though in the arms of her mother. On viewing the remains of his mother Quanah Parker asked Birdsong twice if he were certain that was his mother. The younger man replied he was certain, that the grave had been located by persons who attended the funeral and objects in the burial had been identified beyond a reasonable doubt. To which Quanah replied, "Then I am satisfied, I have looked for her a long time." In compliance with his request, Quanah Parker was buried beside his mother. Mrs. Neda Parker Birdsong wrote the inscription for her father's monument:

> Resting here until day breaks and darkness disappears is Quanah Parker, the last chief of the Comanches. Died Feb. 21, 1911, age 64 years.

There is an annual reunion of the Parker families in memory of Cynthia Ann and Quanah Parker held alternately at Cache, Oklahoma, or Fort Sill and restored Fort Parker. Cynthia Ann Parker was featured in the Texas Independence Centennial program in 1936. In Wichita Falls on April 17, 1951, an audience of two thousand was deeply impressed by the initial production of E.A. Nelson's opera, "Saga of Peta Nocona." A choir of 140 voices from the University of Oklahoma and Midwestern University produced it.

For a child to have to endure the humiliation, anguish, and loneliness of separation from loved ones, coupled with the shock of injection into an alien culture was truly a cruel experience, but for an adult to be compelled to repeat the experience in reverse was an ordeal that might well crush the stoutest heart. The tragic experiences did, however, bring out in an impressive way a characteristic of Cynthia Ann and her son that is inspiring — motherly love and filial devotion. In later years this fact was expressed beautifully in a reburial service. It became expedient to remove the remains of mother and son to Fort Sill, near Lawton, Oklahoma. On this occasion, Major General Thomas E. de Shazo, Commanding General of the United States Artillery and Missile Center, in his funeral oration, as quoted by historian Mildred P. Mayhall, said:

> Her unfailing devotion to her children and Quanah's devotion to her is a part of Southwest history and American tradition. She is a shining example of motherhood in adversity everywhere.

# Margaret Moffette Lea Houston

John French

MARGARET LEA HOUSTON

# Margaret Moffette Lea Houston

by
JAMES M. DAY

During the course of the restless nineteenth century many women made the transference from the comforts offered by Alabama to the unsettled wilds of Texas. The change was not unusual. Even so, Margaret Lea made the move and claimed her fame in a little different manner; she did it by wedding the most famous man in the annals of Texas, none other than Sam Houston. So dominant has he been that her biographers have been unable to extricate her from his political machinations, and even the most definitive story of her life is titled *Sam Houston's Wife*, with the subtitle being *A Biography of Margaret Lea Houston.* Her subjugation was no accident; it was by design during her lifetime. Paradoxically, she was subordinate, yet dominate in her own way.

Margaret Lea was born on April 11, 1819, in what is now Perry County, Alabama, in the west-central part of the state. Alabama was then a territory, having been created only two years prior to her birth, at the same time that the town of Marion, later the county seat of Perry County and Margaret's home, was founded. Interestingly, this Alabama land had once been the habitation of the Choctaw Indians, but it had been forced from them as an aftermath of the Battle of Horseshoe Bend in 1814 and a series of treaties that followed in 1816. Andrew Jackson led the American troops at Horseshoe Bend, while one of his able soldiers was Sam Houston, who received wounds from the battle that were to plague him the remainder of his life. In a strange way the life of Margaret Lea was intertwined with the undulating redland of the prairies of Perry County.

The Lea family had followed a not unusual pattern of migration to Alabama. Margaret Lea's father's ancestors were from England, by way of Virginia, North Carolina, and Georgia, while her grandmother, Lucy Talbert, was from the Huguenots who settled in Georgia. From the marriage of Lucy Talbert and George Lea came nine children, one of whom was Temple Lea, the father of Margaret. Temple Lea married Nancy Moffette, and to them were born seven children as follows: Henry Clinton, Gabriel, Martin, Margaret Moffette, Antoinette Emily, Vernal, and Varilla. Between 1813 and 1816 the Leas moved from Clarke County, Georgia, to the prairies of present Perry County, Alabama.

It was a primitive country as Alabama was then still only a part of the great Mississippi Territory; Alabama Territory was created in 1817; the State of Alabama in 1819, the year Margaret was born. Temple Lea lived until 1834, and in doing so no doubt exerted a strong influence on his children. He was a devout Baptist in an age of fervent revivalism, was a deacon who often preached. His house of worship, Concord Church, was about fifteen miles from the county seat at Marion, but Temple Lea never abandoned it. Even after he settled his family in Marion in 1822, he continued to return to the Concord Church at least once monthly. The remainder of Sundays he worshipped with his family at the Siloam Church in Marion. He was devoted to worship and to the law, proven by the fact that he was appointed the first Probate Judge of Perry County. Likewise, he believed in a good education for his children, females and males alike. He was the man who instructed his children in the rudiments of learning until his death in 1834. He was sixty-one years of age at the time; his daughter, Margaret, was fifteen.

When Temple Lea died, his wife, Nancy, took up the reigns of education for the children with some gusto, and her religious background was no less impressive than her husband's. In 1822, she was a charter member of the Siloam Baptist Church in Marion. The following year she represented the Siloam Missionary Society at the state association meeting at Greensboro, Alabama; then she stayed on to be present for the founding of the Alabama State Convention of the Baptist Church. She was as devotedly religious as her husband, but she had an aspect that was more practical than his. Temple Lea was something of a dreamer, a poet in a way, while Nancy Lea was materialistically oriented. From her family she inherited money which she invested in Alabama land. The cotton plantation developed thereon supported the family and fifty slaves. She was successful, a rather businesslike person who lacked gentleness. She thought she perceived adequately Margaret's introspective nature and did not hesitate to critize the daughter.

Such were the parental influences on Margaret Lea, but they were not the only ones. Her brothers and sisters were of importance. Henry, Martin, and Varilla were over ten years older than Margaret and had children almost as old as the future Mrs. Sam Houston. As Margaret's biographer, William Seale, expressed it "the three oldest Lea children, energetic, ambitious people had long disapproved of the insolent laughter of Antoinette and Vernal and had been protective of the scholarly, introspective Margaret." Henry was a state senator who had a rather impressive house in Marion; it was his house to which, in 1837, the widow Nancy Lea took her three children, Margaret, Vernal, and Antoinette. There Margaret lived for the three years prior to her marriage.

They were troublesome years for her, but she found that Henry's library offered her only solace. Margaret was still visited by a gloominess about her father's death. In the library she found a "favourite resort," a place "Sacred to holy musings and communion with the genius of ages gone by." There, she wrote: "I am in the midst of heroes, ideal and real, sages with their wisdom and philosophy are here and orators and poets with their dusty laurels." Her taste for literature was whetted as she read *Ivanhoe*, *The Naval Foundling, Harry O'Reardon or Illustrations of Irish Pride, Swallow Barn*, and *The Vicar of Wakefield*. Likewise, her bent for poetry and music was accented by her attendance at the Judson Female Institute. In 1839 she penned a poem entitled "A Father," which portrayed her close personal relationship to her father as well as her admiration, respect, and remembrance of his teachings. She wrote:

> Soon I shall sleep within the arms of death.
> Ah then the world will claim for its own,
> And softly woo thee with its poisonous breath!
> Beware! List not the wily flatter's tone!
> 'Twill lead thee onward to despair,
> And leave thy wretched soul to perish there!
>
> Thou heart is formed for love and will entwine
> Its clinging tendrils ever round some stay.
> Poor child, what agony will oft be thine
> To see the prop so trusted torn away.
> But God and faith kindled in thy soul a light,
> Whose radiance ne'er will die, but still shine on
> Undimmed through life, E'en mid the darkest night
> 'Twill shed a lustre o'er the path so lone.
> The love of nature, on a gentle spell
> Within that sacred gift doth ever dwell!
>
> There's beauty too upon thy velvet cheek,
> And softness lies in thou dark blue eyes,
> Ah yes thou'rt fair, but oh be pure and meek,
> And prize thy beauty's glow as thou dost prize
> The flowers that creep along the woodland stream
> The rose that blushes in the valley's shade,
> The evening sky, the twilight's softening gleam,
> Oh ever love all these for him who made,
> And suffer not they gifts bestowed so free,
> To steal thy heart from God who gave them thee!

As she lived in Marion and attended Judson, Margaret Lea received strict religious instruction. Since her father's death she had been troubled with evangelical questions she could not answer, questions which, coupled with her father's death, cast her into deep depression. At age nineteen, during chapel at Pleasant Valley Academy, she found the answers and was converted to religion, and shortly thereafter the Reverend Peter Crawford baptized her as a member of the Siloam Baptist Church. This experience at once pleased the family and gave her life a purpose, one which two years later was transferred to the indomitable Sam Houston.

William Carey Crane first met Margaret Lea in 1839 when she was a student at Judson Female Institute. Crane was a Baptist preacher who remained friends with the Houstons throughout most of their lives. His impression of Margaret as he later recalled it, was that she had "received the best advantages of the schools of Alabama" and that she had associated with "the most cultivated people" in the state. She was "possessed of winning manners and conversational powers," and "she attracted no little attention from men of eminence of Church and State." Crane concluded that "she was regarded as the most attractive and fascinating young lady in that part of Alabama."

Biographer Seale gives additional insight concerning her appearance at that time:

> She was tall, with "beautiful dark brown hair . . . quite full of waves." Her face was an oval with arresting violet eyes. A dauguerrotype of disputed date shows Margaret at perhaps twenty-one or twenty-two. Her hair is parted neatly in the middle and it is shiny, its arrangement forming a long Gothic arch over soft and inquisitive eyes. The silk sleeves are tight at the shoulders, broadening to the wrists in patterns of ribbon and lace. Margaret's expression is grave and old though the picture's general impression is one of a whimsical child. In her diminutive gloved hand she conceals her spectacles, which she kept sewed to her dress by a cord.

Thus, in her educated, religious, secure way, Margaret Moffette Lea grew to womanhood. In May of 1839 Judson Institute recessed for the summer, and Margaret journeyed south to Mobile with her mother to visit other Leas. Antoinette had married William Bledsoe, a wealthy Mobile merchant the previous winter, and Martin Lea also lived there. On an afternoon in May Antoinette gave a party, a strawberry festival, in honor of her mother.

That very afternoon Nancy Lea had an appointment with a man from Texas. It was a business meeting, one arranged because Mrs. Lea had decided to invest in western land. She had made a good profit in selling her Alabama plantation, money she thought would increase if wisely invested. As she looked for outlets, she naturally turned to her son, Martin, who was a successful Mobile promoter. He knew people! One of them was the forty-six-year-old Sam Houston, who happened to be in Mobile in May, 1839, trying to sell some Texas land. Martin Lea thought Houston should talk with Mrs. Lea about the subject. Perhaps Houston could enlighten her.

Sam Houston, sired in Virginia and reared in Tennessee, was famous in both Tennessee and Texas. After an early career as a soldier, he resigned from the army in 1818 to become a lawyer in Lebanon, Tennessee. By October, 1818, he was district attorney and shortly there after he became the state's adjutant general. By 1823, he was a member of the United States House of Representatives, and four years later was elected governor of Tennessee. In 1829, when he resigned as governor, he went to the Cherokee Indians to become a trader. There he took up citizenship, accepted an Indian wife, and drank liquor heavily. In 1832, he entered Texas, the land of his destiny, for thereafter he was connected with most of the political movements that led to Texas' emancipation from Mexico. As commanding general of the Texian Army he was wounded at the Battle of San Jacinto, but recovered to be elected first president of the Republic of Texas, 1836-1838. He was then elected to the Texian Congress, but his responsibilities were greatly lessened, so he expanded his land operations and spent time traveling in the United States to secure money for the ventures. This man had many names: Indians knew him as "The Raven," Texan patriots called him "the Hero of San Jacinto," and his enemies, of whom there were several, labeled him "The Big Drunk." He was, at once, all these things. At age forty-six having a divorce from one wife, having abandoned another, and drinking heavily, he was not a likely candidate for marriage.

They met first in May, 1839, in Mobile, and they married on May 9, 1940, in the home of Henry Lea in Marion. During the days that followed the first meeting, Houston spent some of his time with Nancy Lea in persuading her to interest herself in Texas land; some of the remainder he used to court the youthful Margaret. By the time he left Mobile, Houston had proposed marriage. Nancy Lea did not want her daughter to marry a man so much older, one who had so unsavory a reputation. She finally decided to leave Mobile, taking Margaret with her, but before doing so, she caught Houston while he was down sick and read aloud to him passages from the Bible she thought he should know. Without her mother's permission, Margaret Lea agreed to become the wife of Sam Houston.

Houston wanted an immediate wedding, but Margaret would not agree. Houston, she said, had to visit her family in Marion before a date could be set. He promised to do so in mid-July, but business, or perhaps reluctance to meet a family opposed to the union, prevented him from doing so. In the months that followed a series of letters were exchanged during which Houston asked her to come to Texas for the ceremony and Margaret refused, stating flatly that the Texan would have to come to Alabama for her. She wanted the marriage but wanted it on her own terms. On July 7, 1839, she penned her romantic sentiments:

> We are once more in our native county . . . and I am happy; Quite happy? Ah no— there are those — absent whose station within my heart remains unfilled. Alas, it is ever thus through life! Happiness is a grand union of tender associations, ties and friendships. Let but the smallest of these be removed, and the whole is incomplete . . .
>
> Last night I gazed long upon our beauteous emblem, the *star of my destiny*, and my thoughts took the form of verse, but I will not inscribe them here, for then you might call me a romantic star-struck young lady, and you know I would not like at all to be put in that sublime class of individuals.

When Houston bypassed Marion in returning to Texas, claiming that his country needed him, Margaret replied that she would be waiting for him in Alabama. "Far be it from me," she wrote, "to raise my voice against that of your country! No — if she requires your presence, go without delay! . . . When her cries of oppression are hushed, we will welcome you again to my Native State." She was determined that Sam Houston would not win this battle, and he did not. At last a February wedding was arranged, but it was delayed until April, and finally May.

On May 7, 1840, Houston arrived in Marion by stagecoach from Texas. He was in the uncertain camp of Margaret's relatives. He registered at the Lafayette Hotel, and promptly the wedding was set for May 9, a Saturday morning. The Reverend Peter Crawford performed the ceremony which was followed by a luncheon at the Lafayette. For a week they lived at the hotel as parties were held in their honor. Margaret developed a "mild fever" after the wedding, thus setting a pattern for illness that would be present during much of their married life. During the week a barbeque was held for the Houston's in an oak grove near the Siloam Baptist Church; it was an affair that called for toasts, most of which were for Houston. Major Towns altered the pattern somewhat by offering a salute to Mrs. Houston, whom he addressed as the "Conqueress of the Conqueror." Many doubts may have existed as to the truth of the statement, but time and events eventually proved him right.

The union which had so little promise in it lasted twenty-three years until Houston's death on July 26, 1863. Family and friends of the couple predicted nothing but disaster. Margaret's family saw a man in his late forties, who was a heavy drinker, a non-religious person, a failure at marriage already. Houston's acquaintances were not optimistic either. Ashbel Smith, a particularily close friend, tried to convince Houston that his "temperament" was not quite right for the "quiet of the Cottage." Bernard E. Bee implored him to "resort to any expedient rather than marry." He did this because of Houston's "terrific habits." George W. Hockley was more direct: "This marriage I fear is his death warrant . . . if it ever occurs. Even so far as it is now progressed I shall believe it when I hear that it has been perfected."

To these expressions of doubt Margaret offered one simple sentence as to why: "He had won my heart." Margaret was intent on reforming his drinking habits and on making him one of God's disciples. Sickness and separation developed as two themes of this marriage. The illness was Margaret's problem, the separation Houston's, but throughout it all the devotion of both remained.

When they arrived in Texas, the Houstons stayed temporarily with Nancy Lea in Galveston. They had property at Cedar Point across the bay, but it was too remote so they did not go there. Late in June the separations began. Houston left Margaret at Galveston when he went to Houston City to speak. When he returned he announced that he had accepted other speaking engagements, so Margaret remained with her mother while Houston spent most of the summer politicking. In Galveston she busied herself with social and church activities and with the small cabin made of logs at Cedar Point. The cabin she named "Ben Lomond," and it came to be a place where she went regularly that summer, accompanied by her slaves who worked under her supervision, and by George W. Hockley or Ashbel Smith, both of whom owned farms nearby. Margaret suggested the planting of an oak grove, and that was done, but furniture for Ben Lomond came slowly.

As the summer progressed the conflict between Houston's political life and his marriage came to be more of a problem. Margaret found that the old warrior had reformed somewhat his drinking habits, but she thought that his political movements were not consistent with the promise he had made to withdraw from public life. Selfishly, she attempted to persuade him to devote more time to her and less to politics. Houston demurred, and in so doing announced late in August that he was making a trip to the Redlands, to San Augustine, to take care of his law practice. Margaret decided to go with him, and Houston was pleased. Roads were bad so the trip was a rough one; in preparation Houston borrowed a coach and rented four mules. They went first to Grand Cane, where Antoinette and William Bledsoe lived on their sugar plantation. An overnight stop was planned, but Margaret became ill shortly after entering the house. William Bledsoe had a disease diagnosed as consumption, while Margaret had an acute susceptibility to any disease she heard about. Margaret was ill; Ashbel Smith, her doctor was summoned; he said she was exhausted and could not be moved. Houston was anxious, but he went to San Augustine without her.

As she remained at Grand Cane rumors reached Margaret concerning her husband. Some political enemies charged him with bigamy, others stated that his drinking was worse than ever, while one went so far as to claim that Houston's conduct since his marriage was "beastly and infamous." She heard the charges while she convalesced and wondered if they were true. When she returned to Galveston she wrote to Houston asking if his conduct had been honorable. He replied simply: "My love, I do sincerely hope that you will hear no more slanders of me. It is the malice of the world to abuse me, and really were it not that they reach my beloved Margaret, I would not care one picayune — but that you should be distressed is inexpressible wretchedness to me!"

Toward the middle of November, Houston found Margaret in Galveston, living with her mother. Finally the time had come for the Houston's to establish a home. She wanted to move to Ben Lomond, but he rented a house in Houston City, a town she was not attracted to. In December, when Houston left to journey to Austin as a member of the Congress of the Republic of Texas, Margaret promptly went to Galveston and her mother. The couple had been together less than a month. In Galveston Margaret went into seclusion, spending most of her time reading, resting, and reflecting on the joys of married life. She wrote often to Congressman Houston, stating that she wished he were with her. Bothered about religion, she inserted queries into her letters subtly asking Houston why he was not actively serving the cause of God. Houston, for his part, refused to attend church. Then Margaret's brother Vernal came for a visit, and brother and sister took a short holiday to Houston City. Afterward, Vernal and Nancy Lea went to the Bledsoe's and Grand Cane, leaving Margaret alone in Galveston. She read, worried about Houston's lack of religion, the possibility of his drinking, and walked the beach with her slave, Eliza. She even thought of going to Austin to be with her husband, but he discouraged such an endeavor as being too dangerous.

As the days passed she heard reports that Houston was to be a candidate for the presidency of the Republic, but as late as February he was saying to her that he had "not consented to become a Candidate." He was home again in late February; the Houstons went to Ben Lomond where they stayed together five weeks. Then Houston went to the Redlands to begin his presidential campaign and Margaret went back to her mother. Nancy Lea was moving to Grand Cane to help Antoinette manage the plantation, but Margaret remained in Galveston for a time before following. She heard unkind statements about her husband, but generally ignored them. What she could not ignore was the fact that Sam Houston, instead of getting out of politics, was more deeply involved. Hurt and dejected she traveled to Grand Cane, only to find her mother and sister absorbed in self pity. Margaret was a kindred spirit, but she refused to stay. Abruptly, she and Eliza returned to Galveston to wait for Houston.

By mid-May, 1841, Houston returned. Their marriage was one year old, and they had been together less than one-half of it. Margaret's illnesses had plagued her, but they were only a sample of what was to come. She was happy over Houston's reform about drinking, but he did not attend church and was not too tolerant of her zeal. Still, they both were deeply in love. That summer of 1841 they stayed at Ben Lomond where Margaret entertained the general with her Spanish guitar and with poems she had composed. As Houston summed up the scene: "My dear wife is trying to keep house, and I make a fair hand in the field!" Some political friends visited them completing the domestic picture. Happiness reigned with Margaret until Houston decided in July that he must go to the Redlands to strengthen his political alliances. He wanted Margaret to go with him, but she protested that she was ill. He waited until she was better, then they set a date for departure. Another delay ensued when Margaret became sick on the eve of departure. She remained ill all through August, wrote poetry, and hoped he would not leave. Finally at the end of August he said he would have to leave her; the election was only two weeks away. When she saw that he intended to go without her, Margaret decided she was well enough to travel.

Taking a doctor with them, they traveled for six days in the course of which Margaret observed her husband as he spoke at camp meetings, weddings, balls, and barbecues. They arrived safely at Nacogdoches but had not been there long when the news came that Houston had won a second term as president. Immediately Margaret was in the coach and away to Washington, one hundred miles distant, to participate in a big celebration for her husband. Afterward, in late September, the coach headed back east to San Augustine, where they visited first with Iredell D. Thomas and later with the Philip Subletts. In mid-October they moved on to Nacogdoches to visit with the Adolphus Sterne family and by early November they were back in Houston City for the presidential parade. Margaret was exhausted from the trip even though she had been a distinct success when presented to East Texas society. Adolphus Sterne found her "very agreeable," with a "very intelligent Countenance." He concluded: "though not a brilliant Beuty [sic] I believe the general has a *good* wife." Besides, she was "a first rate musician, on the piano-forte and guitar on which latter instrument she excells."

The new year brought a little more togetherness for the Houstons, but perhaps less healthfulness for Margaret. She was depleted physically from the trip to San Augustine and Nacogdoches. The president stayed with her until December, when he headed off for Austin and his inauguration. Margaret did not go because she delayed the other travelers and because of the expense. Instead, she rested, taking Eliza's herb medicines in an effort to restore her health. She waited in Houston City while Houston struggled in Austin with the possibility of a Mexican invasion. When Congress adjourned in February, 1842, the president rode muleback to Houston City in "two hours less than four days." Margaret was still not well. In late February Houston noted her health when he stated that Margaret's "indisposition" had been such as to "embarrass" him "to some extent." Margaret was a little "on the mend" in March, but worse in April, a condition which added "affliction" to the president's "perplexities."

The Mexican threat coupled with Margaret's ailments caused Houston to send her to Alabama. Accompanied by her brother, Martin, Mrs. Sam Houston went to Marion. She left Texas in May, and she returned in July, but her physical strength did not improve. Chills and headaches persisted, and her doctor, Ashbel Smith, was off to France and England on government business. Even so, Margaret and Sam Houston were together. When the government moved to Washington-on-the-Brazos, the Houstons followed in October, 1842. Margaret visited Grand Cane briefly, then went on to Washington where the Houstons lived with the family of John W. Lockhart.

Mrs. Lockhart crowded her own family into other parts of the house and thus set aside an entire room for the Houstons. Good furniture was placed in the room, but Margaret was not satisfied. Houston placated her seemingly unreasonable demands by closing off the door to the inside of the house and cutting a new entrance to the outside. Margaret then eased her demands a little, but her health was still bad and besides she was pregnant. Houston was ecstatic! He began to give her extra attention, which elated Margaret and caused her to bloom. She went through her pregnancy in a state of seclusion, only rarely appearing out, and then only with Eliza when the two of them took buggy rides into the scenic Brazos prairies. At Christmas Nancy Lea came to take Margaret to Grand Cane for the birthing.

Indeed, the prospective mother was more comfortable at the Bledsoe home, with servants and family to care for her. The only thing missing was Houston. For a few weeks she remained at Grand Cane until Houston appeared to confess that he had taken a bottle of wine from the Lockharts and, having partaken freely thereof, had chopped to pieces a large four-poster bed in the room. It was a confession honestly made, and Margaret, though mortified, was understanding. For example, she understood more clearly that instead of fighting his political career, which had been her "enemy," she must pay extra attention to reforming his drinking habits. She returned to Washington with him, where they rented a small house on the edge of town. Furniture was brought in and they were comfortably settled by early April. Later that month Nancy Lea came to stay, and then word came that Margaret's brother, Martin, had died. With all the upsets, though, Margaret's pregnancy gave her little trouble; she was physically able. The baby born at Washington on May 25, 1843, was named at Margaret's insistance, Sam Houston, Jr. The mother was reasonably content: she had Houston to look after her and her mother and Eliza to see to the house. All she had to do was worry, and guide events to suit her fancy.

This was Margaret's first child, but certainly not her last. Between 1843 and 1860 the couple produced eight children. Sam, Jr. was the first. Then followed Nancy Elizabeth, born September 6, 1946, at Raven Hill near Huntsville; Margaret Lea, born April 13, 1848, at Huntsville; Mary William, born April 9, 1850, at Huntsville; Antoinette Power, born January 20, 1852, at Huntsville; Andrew Jackson born June 21, 1954, at Independence; William Rogers, born May 25, 1858, at Huntsville, and Temple Lea, born August 12, 1860, in the Governor's Mansion at Austin. Obviously, the places of birth reflect the various places the family lived for the seventeen year period; that is, where Margaret lived, for the general was not always there. Nor were all of Margaret's pregnancies as easy as the first one.

From the time Sam Houston, Jr., was born until Sam Houston, Sr., rode away to the United States Senate on March 9, 1846, a period of thirty-three months, the Houstons followed their usual pattern of separation. They were together eighteen months and a few days; apart for almost fourteen months. Even so, their devotion one for the other held strong, and much happened. For example, Houston had promised Margaret a carriage, a promise he kept by ordering a barouch from New Orleans. Designed with four seats, the coach was painted bright yellow, and it came to be a Texas conversation piece. It was not what the lady had in mind, not so elegant as she wanted, but Margaret seems not to have complained.

She and Sam, Jr., spent much of the year 1844 at Grand Cane with her sister Antoinette. Houston spent his time establishing order in the Redlands, making treaties with Indians, and campaigning for Anson Jones for president. Margaret spent hers making friends with the other residents along the Trinity River, going to picnics, and organizing a Baptist church. Her mother and Antoinette were her companions. She especially liked to go to the Ellis place down the river where Nancy Lea, Antoinette, and Margaret heard Mr. Ellis read from the Bible. Afterward, Margaret played the guitar and they all sang hymns. Her letters to the president did not stress physical ailments; she seems to have been content.

Finally, Houston's term as President of the Republic was ended on December 9, 1844, as he and Margaret were reunited. She was so pleased!! At last Houston was out of politics she thought. So elated was she that she penned a poem to him entitled "My Husband." She wrote:

> Dearest, the cloud hath left thy brow,
> The shade of thoughtfulness, of care,
> And deep anxiety; and now
> The sunshine of content is there.

Its sweet return with joy I hail;
And never may thy country's woes
Again that hallowed light dispel
And thy bosom's calm repose.

God hath crowned thy years of toil
With full fruition; and I pray,
That on the harvest still His smile
May shed its ever glad'ning ray.

Thy task is done; another eye
Than thine, must guard thy country's weal;
And Oh! may wisdom from on high
To him the one true path reveal.

When erst was spread the mighty waste
Of water fathoms wide and far
And darkness rested there, unchased
By ray of sun or moon or star.

God bade the gloomy deep recede
And so young earth rose on His view
Swift at His word the waters fled
And darkness spread his wings and flew.

The same strong arm hath put to flight
Our country's foes - the ruthless band
That swept in splendid pomp and might
Across our fair and fertile land.

The same almighty hand hath raised
On these wild plains a structure fair
And well wondering nations gaze
At aught so marvelous and rare.

Thy task is done. The holy shade
Of calm retirement waits thee now,
The lamp of hope relit hath shed
Its sweet refulgence o'er thy brow.

Far from the busy haunts of men
Oh! may thy soul each fleeting hour
Upon the breath of prayer ascend
To him who rules with love and power.

All was bliss. Outside the small town of Huntsville, Houston had purchased a tract of land where he had instructed his slave, Joshua, to build a cabin. Using the yellow coach Margaret and her husband journeyed forth to the place, named Raven Hill, to finally make a home worthy of the name.

The two large square rooms were made of pine logs squared by axe, and the windows were protected only by shutters. Outside, in a fenced area, was the kitchen and a place for Margaret to plant flowers. The Houstons, nestled in the pines, centered their life around Sam, Jr., who, according to one observer, was "thoroughly the pride" of both parents.

Yet, a restlessness remained with the general. Texas' annexation to the United States was the big political question of the day, and Houston could not long avoid it. At the end of April the yellow coach rumbled away from Raven Hill heading to Grand Cane. When they arrived, Houston found from newspapers that he was embroiled with the annexation fight. As a result, he wrote letters and scheduled speeches which took him to Houston City and Galveston. Margaret, by now reasonably accustomed to his moods, had lost him again, not to drink this time but to politics. She stayed at the Bledsoe's where work was enthusiastically being done to organize the Concord Baptist Church, obviously named for the old home church in Alabama. Among the seven founders of the church were Nancy Lea, Antoinette Bledsoe, and Margaret Houston. Houston had arrived three days prior to the church's founding, and he had wanted to leave with Margaret for the United States, but Margaret thought her work for God was more important than his political involvements.

After the ceremony the Houstons went to Galveston, sailed for New Orleans, journeyed to Nashville, and finally visited Andrew Jackson's home, The Hermitage. Margaret and Sam Houston arrived about four hours after the death of "Old Hickory." As they visited the death room, Sam Houston held his son and admonished the youth to try to remember that he had gazed upon the face of Andrew Jackson. One wonders about the emotions of Margaret. Afterward, Houston attracted much attention, while Margaret was pleased to go into seclusion at Tulip Grove, the home of Andrew Jackson Donelson. Well into August they stayed there. Margaret passed the time by visiting the mourning members of Jackson's family and by visiting religious persons in the neighborhood. The Houstons went to Blount Springs, Alabama, for mineral baths and then on to Marion where Margaret remained while Houston went back to Texas. This separation lasted four months.

In Marion, Margaret lived with her brother, Henry, in the same house where she had spent her childhood. She stayed there rather than return to Texas because she felt that Sam, Jr., should become acquainted with his Alabama relatives. Besides, the general was busy with politics and with work on Raven Hill. In January, 1846, she was at Grand Cane, where she waited for Houston. Concord Baptist Church was being built as he came to her in late January. The following Sunday, Margaret was proud as a peacock as she and Sam Houston walked out to attend church. With this victory, she was indeed a conqueress.

Houston himself had analyzed the situation only two months prior to the event. Writing to a cousin, William H. Letcher, the Raven described his marriage:

> . . . It has been my lot to be happily united, to a wife that I love, and so far, we have a young scion of the old stock. . . . I hope he will be a useful, and pious man. It will be the happiest destiny for the Boy.
>
> My wife is pious, and her great desire is, that Sam should be reared, in the fear, and admonition of the Lord. It is likewise my desire. Not because my wife desires it, and controls me (as the world has it) but, for sundry weighty reasons. You have, I doubt not, heard that my wife controls me, and has reformed me, in many respects? This is pretty true, and I tell her, that I am willing that she should have the full benefit of my character, but it so happens, that she gets all the credit for my good actions, and I have to endure, all the censure of my bad ones. Thus you see, that I am bankrupt, in all good reputation. Well, so long as a good name remains in the family, I will be satisfied.

Houston may have attended church, but he did not abandon politics. He was elected a United States Senator in February as he and Margaret were back at Raven Hill enjoying domestic tranquility. At first she was going to Washington with him, but then she discovered she was pregnant again. Houston went to Washington in March, while Margaret remained at Raven Hill. From 1846 to 1859 Houston was a senator, and as such about half of his time was spent either in Washington or in Texas politicking. Moments found Margaret with him, but they were rare, so she savored them. One of the children later said the house had a circus-like atmosphere when Houston came home because he was there so seldom.

Margaret resided first at Raven Hill and then in a house in Huntsville until 1853. Between 1853 and 1856 the home was at Independence, ostensibly so the children could attend college. The summer of 1856 was spent at Cedar Point; then Margaret was deposited back in Huntsville. She was waiting there when Houston returned from Washington to become Governor of Texas. Letters in profusion flowed between the lady and her senator, letters which depict family problems and solutions and which reveal the constancy of their love. Houston started attending church in Washington rather regularly, and Margaret was overjoyed. He did it he said out of respect for his wife who was "one of the best Christians on earth." He was not always punctual in his church attendance, and when he was not, Margaret chided him in her letters. Finally, in November, 1854, her dream was realized; Sam Houston was baptized into the church. Margaret's biographer, William Seale, captured the essence of her relationship to the event when he wrote:

> At noon the hero of San Jacinto stumbled from the cold water into the cheering conflux that swept forward to congratulate him. Margaret could hardly see him for all the people. But it was her custom to stay back. She never interfered with Sam Houston and his public. Experience had taught her to wait until the people were gone, when he would come to her of his own accord.

The scene suggests that Margaret had attained much understanding about the kind of man she had married and had adjusted to the situation. She had reformed his drinking habits, had led him to be converted to Christianity, but she could do nothing about his politics. She was wise enough to leave that alone. Still, with this growth on her part, she was not well. In February 1847, she had a pain in her breast that was so severe that she summoned Dr. Asbel Smith from Galveston to see about it. Smith came, performed an operation to remove the cancer, and she was able to walk a little when Houston got home in April. Intermittently, she was ill for much of the thirteen years her husband served in the United States Senate. Perhaps contributing to the condition was the fact she bore six children during that time.

Through all the illness, and through the separation, their devotion for each other did not fade. This aspect of Margaret remained unchanged. In the beginning she was addressing letters to him as "My beloved;" in the end it was still the same. She expressed it in 1846 as follows:

> As we expect Maj. McDonald today, I have thought it best, to prepare a letter to go by him, but I do most sincerely hope, that when you read it, I shall be sitting, as in bye gone days, on your lap, with my arms around your neck, the happiest, the most blest of wives. Do not suppose that I intend to surprise you with a visit, and get to you before the letter. No — it is not that, but as Maj. M's route will be a tedious one, I do indeed hope, that before he can get to Washington, you will have left the city, for home, and consequently, when my letter returns, as of course it will do so, you may have some curiosity to know what I said to you, when you were far away. I may be dreaming of bliss, never, never to be realized, but hope is whispering softly, in my ear, and dropping sweetness from its dewy wings upon this lone, lone heart. Who would not listen to so sweet a charmer! I often reproach myself severely, for wishing to hurry the moments of your absence, the precious moments given me, to prepare for eternity, and I have no excuse for this sinful impatience, except that my husband is so inexpressably dear to me, that I cannot be happy without him. Alas "the time is short," and "in that day," nothing will serve as an excuse, for having defrauded our Heavenly Master of a single moment that was his due. Should we meet again, oh, may the main business of our lives be, to prepare for Heaven!

The feeling was still as strong when he was finally home.

Another incident, the one about Virginia Thorne, illustrates another aspect of Margaret's character. Virginia Thorne was a youth seven years of age when she came into Margaret's life by way of her brother, Vernal and his wife, Mary. The couple had been made Virginia's guardians by a court in Galveston. When she was brought to Grand Cane, Margaret was there. Margaret was also present when Virginia defied the wrath of Nancy Lea and was about to be spanked with a yowpon switch before Vernal and Mary intervened. In time, when Mary became a semi-invalid, she asked Margaret to take charge of Virginia if she, Mary, died before the youth was of age. Margaret agreed, and eventually Virginia came under her tutelage. The trouble was rather immediate.

First came the mysterious "poisoning" incident with Sam, Jr. Then came the involvement with Thomas Gott, the overseer Margaret had hired while Houston was in Washington. Virginia was fourteen, Gott twenty-six, but they spent time together and they infuriated Margaret. The gossip was that Gott and Virginia were intimate. Margaret's piety was not able to take such talk; a break had to come. The climax arrived one night when Nancy Elizabeth (Nannie) was being put to bed. Nannie was so playful that Virginia jerked her from the bed to the floor. Margaret, seeing what happened, picked out a cowhide whip and hit Virginia on the arms, back, and shoulders about twenty times. Virginia had cuts on her right elbow and her wrist when it was over, but the beating calmed her. Margaret had no more trouble with her until about one month later when, in later January, 1850, Virginia and Gott eloped. Margaret felt she had been "faithful" to her trust; she was pleased that Virginia Thorne was gone. Pleased that is until June when Virginia and Gott filed charges of assault and battery against her.

Senator Houston sustained his wife, and even defended her to their children. Didactically, he wrote to Sam, Jr.:

> Bad men, and bad women, are the only beings that will not return good for good and kindness, for kindness. You will not like to be compared to bad people, who only love themselves, and wish to see, other people unhappy. Bad or wicked people cannot be happy, and they wish to see others unhappy, that they may be like them. The wicked are bad, because they are the children of the Devil, and not children of light. Sin is compared to darkness, because in darkness we can see no pleasant thing, and goodness is compared to light, because we can see, and enjoy all good things. Heaven is light and joy; God made light, and His throne is in light. He made darkness also, but it was for the wicked.
>
> ... Learn, my son, to be good. You are a blessed Boy, because while you are young, you have a kind Mother to teach you to be good, and pray with you, and for you!

In late September the grand jury heard the case but could not decide it. There was a tie vote, so the case was referred to the Baptist church where Margaret was fully acquitted. Both Margaret and Houston thought the court action was caused by Houston's political enemies.

Margaret Houston became the "First Lady" of Texas in 1859 when Sam Houston won his last political race. Already she had been the "President's Lady" early in their marriage, but things were different when Texas was a republic. Margaret then had been full of reform, seeking to change Houston's character. Now, in December, 1859, the adjustments had been made as he was inaugurated. She did not care where they lived so long as they were together. From mid-December, 1859, to March 19, 1861, they occupied the governor's mansion in Austin. Houston had many problems with the government, but the biggest one, the one that finally drove the family from the mansion, was Texas' secession from the Union.

For her part, Margaret chose to live a life of seclusion. As was her way, she was protective about her family and kept them out of public view as much as possible. She was expecting her eighth child so she withdrew from society, a retreat that was to remain while they resided at the mansion. She had passed her fortieth birthday, had borne eight children, and had lived half of her life in an atmosphere that approached frontier-like conditions. Her seclusion has made description of her at this time difficult. One of her nephews stated that she was "beyond the measurement that Grecian artists gave to their sculptured statues of goddesses." Her gracefulness, he thought, resulted from a "mysterious charm." Her hair had gray streaks in it and she still parted it in the middle. Otherwise little is known of her looks.

Of her presence there can be little doubt. When Governor Houston was backed into a corner on the issue of the oath of loyalty to the Confederacy, he sat up the night of March 15, 1861, pondering his decision. Would he take the oath or not? When his wife came to him the next morning he turned to her with the words, "Margaret, I will never do it." Three days later when the legislature declared the office of governor vacant, Margaret started packing. Late in March the yellow coach, Margaret inside, led the Houstons and their possessions out of Austin and on to Independence. Margaret had just turned forty-two; Houston was sixty-eight.

Aging but still restless, Houston allowed Margaret to remain at Independence for two months, then he had to go to Cedar Point. Twenty-one years of marriage had increased Margaret's mobility, so the couple and the younger children returned to Cedar Point and Ben Lomond, the cabin decorated to be their bridal suite. The household routine was set to please Houston; Margaret did it deliberately. Even so, Houston visited in Galveston and Houston City as much as he could, leaving Margaret to her loneliness and her Bible. Her illnesses increased, but her husband would not remain at home; when he returned she entertained him as best she could. Worries about the children and about the fortunes of Texas and the Confederacy were, in addition to the Bible, topics of conversation and concern.

In October, 1862, the family left Cedar Point for Independence, but they stayed there only a while before moving to the Steamboat House at Huntsville. Margaret was not pleased with the thought of going back to Huntsville, but she did it because it was what he wanted. The Steamboat House was her home for almost a year. She fixed up the place to suit their needs, particularly those of Sam Houston who was becoming feeble. She saw to the children, but shielded her husband from bad news about them. The war bothered him, so he went to the coast again, to Galveston and Houston, where he spoke publicly. This was in March, 1863, when he was just past seventy years of age. When he went back to Margaret at the Steamboat House, he was sick. Indians came to visit him, and Margaret, who was not fond of the redmen, tolerated them as they sat at Houston's feet in an effort to cheer him. Then she persuaded him to go to Sour Lake for mud baths, and she even threatened to move to the dry lands of the west in an effort to prolong his life.

He returned again to Huntsville in late June, but his illness became worse. Margaret cared for him diligently, and even Ashbel Smith, their doctor, came to examine him. It was all for nought. His death came on July 26, 1863, as Margaret sat beside his bed and read to him from the Bible. His last words were, "Texas . . . Margaret — Margaret." Those were the two things on earth that he loved the most. One supposes that it happened the way Margaret wanted; she had conquered everything about Sam Houston except death, and her Bible took care of that.

Margaret stayed on at the Steamboat House until November. Then she decided to return to Independence. Money was a problem to her now, for even though Houston had left her thousands of acres of land, she had no cash. In managing, she sold much of the land. At Independence she lived with her mother until Nancy Lea died on the morning of February 7, 1864. Margaret did not have the strength to attend the funeral. She concerned herself with money matters and with her children, but she still found her peace in her Bible. Margaret was as retiring as ever as she sat and read and prayed. She did become good friends with the Baptist preacher and his wife, Catherine and William Carey Crane, and she opened Houston's archives to Crane and persuaded him to write a biography of Houston which detailed his "religious character."

As the months passed, the older children married and moved away, the war ended, and the lines of care showed more pronouncedly in Margaret's face. At age forty-eight in 1867 her body had become heavier since Houston had died, and her hair was "combed and tucked for practicality rather than appearance." Her primary duty lay with the two younger boys, William Rogers and Temple who were eleven and seven respectively, and who needed to be reared as their father wished. By his will they were to be taught early "an utter contempt for novels and light reading." Particular attention was to be given to the development of their "morals." Such were the guidelines given Margaret, and she did her best as money and strength provided. Margaret was not long on either.

Starting in September, 1867, an epidemic of yellow fever spread across Texas. When it reached Independence, most of the town was silent except for the rattle of the death wagon as it clattered to the cemetery. Margaret got away from the plague by going to Labadie Prairie where her daughter, Maggie, lived with her family. In early December she was going to Georgetown, Texas, to spend Christmas with her daughter Nannie and family, but she remembered some items she wanted to pick up at her house in Independence. She traveled in her yellow coach. At home she was packing, for she thought to stay a long time at Georgetown. The fever struck her, she was sick for two days before her death on December 3, 1867. A long time family friend, Major E. W. Cave, a servant named Bingley, and two of her children, Nettie and Mary Willie, buried her. No one else was around — a minister did not even conduct services.

Yet, if all went according to her plan, she was again united with Sam Houston and this time he could not go drinking or politicking, and her health would not need to be considered.

# Elisabet Ney

ELISABET NEY

# Elisabet Ney

by
DORMAN H. WINFREY

Arthur Schopenhauer, the great German philosopher remarked that if you did not know the sculptress Ney "you have lost a great deal."

Lorado Taft, American sculptor and art critic, said "Elisabet Ney is one of the most interesting of characters as she is one of the best equipped of women sculptors." Mrs. Bride Neill Taylor, Austin resident and one-time president of the Texas State Historical Association, considered Elisabet Ney "the pioneer in the art development of Texas" and said "the day on which she entered the capitol city of Texas marks a new era in the development of the state."

Born in Muenster, Westphalia, Germany, on January 26, 1833, Elisabet Ney was the daughter of Johann Adam and Elisabet (Wrenze) Ney. Her mother's family had a Polish background and her father was a relative of Napoleon's Marshal Michel Ney. The family also consisted of two other children, a brother and a sister.

As a child, Elisabet was apparently fascinated by the work of her father, an artisan who had a reputation of sorts for statues for cemeteries and religious figures. This early contact with the art of sculpture doubtless influenced her choice of a life's work. In addition, the child was to take on the individuality of dress that had characterized her father. The hat and cloak that he designed for himself and wore with little regard for fashion may have inspired her preference for flowing gowns in preference to whalebone and other appurtenances of nineteenth century attire.

At the age of eighteen, Elisabet Ney stunned and shocked her parents when she announced that she was going to Berlin to study the art of sculpture. Such a proposal was unthinkable. The profession was open only to men, and there were only men teachers. Not only was the work itself physically demanding, but also there was nowhere that a woman could study anatomy as she would need to. Her mother worried for fear such a venture would wreck her daughter's Catholic faith. Thus when the daughter threatened to go on a hunger strike, the local bishop was called in to help persuade the rebellious teenager to change her mind. But the bishop was as defeated as the parents and recommended that the young girl be given permission to leave Muenster and go away to school. A slight compromise was won by the parents and the bishop when Elisabet agreed to go to

Munich, a strong Catholic center, instead of the Protestant Berlin. For Elisabet, the move was only a delay. She was still determined to study under the leading sculptor of the day, Christian Rauch.

★ ★ ★

Thus began the first of the three distinct periods of Elisabet Ney's adult life. As a student and young artist she was to gain considerable success in the years between 1851 and 1870. From 1870 until the late 1880's she did virtually no artistic work. From 1890 until her death in 1907 she again was producing sculpture, the first in Texas.

Much of what we know about the German sculptor's life is from *Elisabet Ney, Sculptor*, published by Bride Neill Taylor of Austin, in 1916. While the limited number of documents available strain the credibility of some of the recollections that the artist passed on to the author, that she told the stories tells something about Elisabet Ney. And they also tell much about the impression that the German sculptor made upon Texans when she arrived in the post Civil War period.

That the spirit of these recollections if not all the details is correct is indicated by I.K. Stephens' *Hermit Philosopher of Liendo*, a biography of Edmund Montgomery that was published in 1951 and that is based on considerable research in several sources including the papers of Montgomery now housed at Southern Methodist University.

★ ★ ★

In Munich, Elisabet lived in the home of a friend of her mother's. When she asked for entrance to the Academy of Art in 1852, she was at first refused before being admitted "on trial." She had no trouble succeeding as a student, and while she was enrolled in the Academy all sorts of safeguards were provided for her. Every day a professor came and got her and walked with her to the Academy, and, no doubt, she must have been the center of attention in the classroom.

A most significant event took place in Heidelberg in 1852 when she first saw Edmund Montgomery, who was to become her "friend," companion, and husband. Montgomery, who was of Scottish parentage but had been educated by private tutors prior to becoming a student of medicine at the University of Heidelberg, had a brilliant mind as well as something else strongly in his favor: he had been a participant in the revolutionary uprising during 1848 and helped build the barricades. Revolutionary Ney had met her hero. At the time, Montgomery, not yet twenty, "was very tall, very slim, very straight, carried himself with the easy grace and confidence and the high head which, to her mind, bespoke a very prince of youth clad in black velvet with abundant blond curly hair falling to his broad shoulders."

Perhaps, it was not surprising that these two should have met. She was beautiful; he, handsome. Both had brilliant minds and were rebels and idealists with "no choice but to love one another." Unfortunately, the pair also shared "a truly tragic incapacity for the practical." Elisabet was not interested in marriage because this would interfere with her life's ambition. She would not marry Edmund Montgomery but would take him on as her "best friend."

Elisabet Ney and Edmund Montgomery must have thrived on the life in Munich. The city was the center for art, music, literature, science, philosophy and political experiment. The two "not only read and studied romanticism at one of its fountain heads, they lived it." In Munich, Elisabet became acquainted with the important people, and one of her close friends was Cosima, daughter of Franz Liszt.

Elisabet Ney still had her eyes set for Berlin and in 1854 felt that the time had come to make "an assault upon the fortress." She was ready to study under the great Christian Rauch who was advancing in age. But Rauch was a producer of great works and not primarily a teacher of students. Could this old man, however, refuse to take on this young student who at the time was "very tall and slender, sculpturesque — even classic in the effect she produced — white, white as milk, with a mass of short auburn curls all over her head. Dressed oftenest in white lace, and carrying herself with the calm poise of a queen, but with far more independence than any queen ever dared to show; yet, in spite of this, full of a lovely grace of manner and a soft sweetness which hid the warrior-like fibre of her secret soul." In speaking, she had "a most delicately played flute, yet with depth and strength also, and used with a perfection of modulation seldom heard."

Rauch would not accept the young student immediately but requested that she submit a composition of her work that he could examine. When she complied with his wishes, he was sufficiently impressed with her work to invite her to occupy a studio next to his. Rauch then recommended Elisabet Ney for the honor of scholarship at the Berlin Academy of Art. This was also a man's world and no place for a girl, but entry she did obtain and was on her way to conquering Berlin as she had Munich. One other female student was in the school at that time, a member of the royal family of Prussia who later became the Empress Freidrich, mother of the later Kaiser William II. The royal student treated Elisabet with total indifference during the time they were both in the Academy.

In 1859, Elisabet Ney gained great fame when she executed the bust of Arthur Schopenhauer. This world renowned figure was the "most talked of, most sought after . . . the most tantalizing of all the lions. . ." People from all over the world desired the opportunity and privilege of Schopenhauer's companionship but very few had access to him. Elisabet used the direct approach to conquer the old philosopher. She went to his apartment in Frankfort and gained entry, though very few had been able to penetrate "the inner sanctum of greatness." She persuaded the elderly man to sit for her and, no doubt, with her youth, beauty and charm brought a certain pleasure to the old man. He later remarked that the sculptress was "very beautiful . . . charming . . . I did not believe that there existed such a charming girl."

And Schopenhauer had great influence on Elisabet Ney. He reinforced her opposition to contemporary social customs and abetted Edmund Montgomery's efforts to influence Elisabet Ney to renounce her own religious beliefs.

By the time Rauch died in 1857 and Schopenhauer in 1860, Elisabet Ney had securely established a reputation in the German world of art. Before 1870, she sculpted busts or bas-reliefs of Alexander von Humboldt, Jacob Grimm, Cosima Liszt, Arthur Schopenhauer, Garibaldi, Bismarck, King George V (last king of Hanover), King Ludwig II of Bavaria, and numerous other distinguished figures.

Certainly all of these persons had strong reputations and through their acquaintance and associations Elisabet Ney's fame grew as did her fortunes. People knew that she was one of Rauch's students, and it became appropriate when famous people wanted a bust done to engage Elisabet Ney, "Rauch's favorite pupil." Elisabet Ney "the young girl from Muenster" had made it in the big league of art, and her home town in 1862 invited her to come back and execute some statues of local heroes to be placed on a new town hall. Unfortunately these figures were destroyed by Allied bombing during World War II.

As Elisabet Ney's career was making great gains in the artistic world, Edmund Montgomery was studying medicine, obtaining the firm grounding in physiology that would enable him to continue his research after he reached Texas. He studied at Heidelberg from 1852-1855, spent 1855-1856 in Berlin, was in Bonn 1856-1857 and in 1858 took his medical degree from Wurzburg. His studies and residency took him to Prague and Vienna. From 1860-1863, he held positions with hospitals in England and became a member of the Royal College of Physicians of London. When a tubercular infection forced him to leave London, he moved to Madeira, at the time, a favorite playground and health resort of the European aristocracy, where he soon built a thriving medical practice. Elisabet Ney was also there as the companion of her "best friend," (biographers differ on whether she arrived before or after Montgomery). Dr. Montgomery pointed out to Elisabet that such circumstances involving the two would doubtless create gossip and almost certainly offend his patients. This time — one of the few occasions in their life — he took a stand and forced her to submit. She agreed to marriage and the two of them went to the English Consulate, where they were married on November 7, 1863. Both gave the age of twenty-eight.

Although Elisabet had agreed to a legal marriage, she made few changes in her way of life. (After the marriage, she sent Dr. Montgomery to his residence and she went to hers at a local hotel.) Dr. Montgomery, in good financial circumstances then, provided a villa where they could both live and she could have her own studio. She still controlled the situation, however, and directed that he would occupy one part of the place and she another. Her area would be off-limits for her "best friend." Most important, she was to be called Miss Ney rather than Mrs. Montgomery; perhaps she felt entitled to use her professional name, a common practice accepted today.

The summer of 1866 found the two romantics spending time in a castle in the Austrian Tyrol. Most significantly, a housekeeper Crescentia Simath met the Montgomerys. Only two years older than Elisabet and Edmund, "Cencie," as she came to be known, would spend her life in service to the Montgomerys, accompanying them not only to other places in Europe but also America. During the time in Austria, the Montgomerys were attempting to make contact with Garibaldi, the great Italian patriot, and "Cencie" is said to have taken the messages exchanged between the parties. Contact was made and as a result Elisabet Ney visited Garibaldi in September, 1866, on the island of Caprera and executed a bust and statuette of the Italian hero.

When Elisabet and Edmund returned to Munich in 1867, much gossip surrounded their activities. Elisabet had changed her ways not at all. She maintained a separate residence and her husband referred to her as "Fraulein Ney." The Germans were unsure of the pair's marital status. Fame, nevertheless, continued to come to Elisabet Ney's studio. From the King of Prussia (he would later become the first German emperor), came a commission to do a bust of Bismarck. When the City of Munich wanted to pay honor to the noted chemist Justus von Liebig with an appropriate gift, his request was for the work she later named "Sursum" done in her studio at Madeira. And other great persons of the world came to her with commisssions. Ludwig II, "Mad King of Bavaria," who had a reputation as a patron of the arts, commissioned her to do a bust of him. This was, perhaps, one of her finest achievements. She was given a place to work in the palace, but the King's growing preoccupation with his deteriorating mental health frustrated her work. The story is told that when Ludwig sent Elisabet Ney a collection of jewels to show his appreciation for her work, she told him "I have no time to care for jewels, Your Majesty. When my friends wish to make me gifts, they send me flowers." The King then ordered his gardeners to cut flowers from his own royal gardens and deliver them to Miss Ney's studio.

Miss Ney's role in the intrigue that surrounded Ludwig's court is unknown. As a sculptor she first met Garibaldi and then through him apparently received a commission to do a bust of Bismarck. Whether her commission in Bavaria was one of Bismarck's efforts to gain the acquiescence of Ludwig II in unification of the German states is unknown. It is known that she quarrelled at this time with her old friend Cosima Liszt when Cosima left her husband, Hans von Bulow, and went to live with Richard Wagner, one of the favorites in Ludwig's court. Whether this quarrel was over morals or politics is unclear. In any case, as the situation worsened, Miss Ney and Dr. Montgomery made plans to slip away quietly during the Christmas season of 1870. They may have been unhappy over the circumstances which resulted from the Franco-Prussian War that year. After stopping briefly to visit her parents, they set sail from Bremen. When the pair and Cencie arrived in New York, they quickly set out for Thomasville, Georgia, where Baron Vicco von Stralendorff, a friend of Montgomery's, and his wife had settled in hopes of allaying the Baron's symptoms of tuberculosis.

Although there may have been plans to establish a community of Germans in the area, no such colony materialized. In fact, after an epidemic of malaria, the Baron and his wife returned to her family's home in the summer and later returned to Germany where the Baron died. During the second summer in America, Miss Ney and Dr. Montgomery set out for a tour of the East and Mid-West though the doctor's tuberculosis made it impossible for him to live in a harsh climate. During the first years in the United States two sons, Arthur and Lorne, were born to the couple.

In 1873, Miss Ney set out for Texas, where she was enchanted with Liendo, a plantation house near Hempstead, that had fallen into disrepair in the years since the Civil War. A magnificent sixteen room, two-story home in provincial Greek revival style, Liendo was one of the historic old homes of Texas. It was begun in 1853 by Leonard Groce, son of one of Stephen F. Austin's original colonists. "Groce's Plantation" is one of the most frequently mentioned centers of activity in the early years of Texas independence, and was the site of a post office during the Republic. Construction of Liendo was a huge undertaking; lumber had to be shipped to Texas from Georgia, and brought overland from Galveston by ox-drawn wagons. Bricks for the foundation had to be made by hand from the clay of the Brazos River banks. Liendo in ante bellum days was known as a center of culture and hospitality. Confederate troops were quartered there during the Civil War, and General George A. Custer occupied the grounds during Reconstruction.

The Liendo Plantation was exactly suited to the needs and temperaments of Miss Ney and Dr. Montgomery. He had space to set up a laboratory where he could conduct his experiments, and she had ideal conditions in which to bring up her two sons, an activity to which she now devoted herself. Both were no doubt captivated by the romantic atmosphere lent the place by the huge grove of trees surrounding it. After she went into the house, Miss Ney is supposed to have said, "Here is where I shall live and die" and on May 4,

1873, the couple paid the $10,000 price for the place that was to be their final home.

The prospect of building an estate as well as molding the flesh and blood of her sons filled Miss Ney with an ambition as strong as that which had begun her career as a sculptor. Unfortunately, the task was to be impossible for her. During the first summer at Liendo, Arthur, then three, contacted diphtheria and died. Dr. Montgomery was in the East at the time of the boy's death, and the mother cremated the body and kept the ashes until they were buried with Dr. Montgomery after his death. Neighbors had already speculated about the man who called the mother of his children "Miss Ney." And the rumors of what had happened chilled them. For many years stories have been told and retold about the cremation of Arthur. Evidence is now available that Dr. Conway Raleigh Nutt, who attended Arthur, "persuaded Elisabet Ney to have the child cremated to prevent the spread of diphtheria in that part of the country." No doubt it took a brave and courageous mother to carry out the doctor's orders.

At Liendo, the division of labor within the household was similar to what it had been in Georgia. Cencie managed the house, Miss Ney ran the farm, and Dr. Montgomery pursued the experiments in his laboratory and the writing of articles for scientific journals. Although many of Miss Ney's problems resulted from her lack of skill as a farmer, she was not the only one who fell on hard times. Almost all farmers were having trouble, a fact proved by the political unrest of the period.

★ ★ ★

Several questions about Miss Ney's life in Texas provide grounds for interesting speculation. Although she sought the advice of Julius Runge, German Consul at Galveston, upon her arrival, Miss Ney seems already to have decided that she wanted a Southern plantation home that could be purchased for a price she could afford in the most highly cultivated German settlement. Runge gave her a letter of introduction to Robert Leisewitz, a cotton broker who lived at Brenham. It was he who showed her Liendo, which was located in Waller County to the east of most of the German settlements.

During the years after her arrival at Liendo, a railroad was finally constructed to San Antonio; and Germans in the area began to have considerable impact on the cultural life of what had been the state's largest city during the period when Texas belonged to Spain and Mexico. Although there are records that Miss Ney visited San Antonio, it is somewhat surprising that she did not become a part of this cultural life. Certainly ties with Germany were close enough that many of the German residents must have known of her European reputation. Because of growing interest in medicine in San Antonio, doubtless residents there would have been impressed by the academic credentials of her husband. Although his interest seems always to have been in physiology as applied to his philosophical research rather than practice, he was a graduate of German medical education as well as a member of the Royal Academy of Physicians in London.

★ ★ ★

Although they sank further and further in debt each year, it was to be Lorne who brought matters to a head. Although both parents were geniuses, Lorne was not. There was a decided generation gap and most probably he was overprotected as a child. Responding violently to the realization that people in the neighborhood considered him and his family "different" (he had a governess and was dressed in Little Lord Fauntleroy clothes), he was rapidly becoming unmanageable — with much of the fury being directed to his mother for whom he blamed this difference. Perhaps for the first time since he had told Elisabet on Madeira that they must be legally married, Dr. Montgomery took a firm stand. Lorne would be sent away to school. Shortly before his departure, Miss Ney sculpted a bust — one of the few pieces she had produced since her arrival in Texas — of her son. In later years, rather than admit that it was of Lorne, she told visitors to her studio that it was an idealization. Perhaps it was.

In 1878, Miss Ney and Dr. Montgomery had become acquainted with Oran M. Roberts when he visited Hempstead while campaigning for the governorship. He was interested in her work, and Miss Ney — who had received most of her more important commissions from governments in Europe — was interested in the possibilities that support from him might open up. Although Roberts' hopes for work by the German sculptor in the new Capitol came to naught when no funds were included for sculpture, it was he who was largely responsible for the commission that came in the 1880's.

As a member of the committee to provide something appropriate relating to Texas for the World's Columbian Exposition at Chicago in 1893, former Governor Roberts contacted Miss Ney. Although compensation for the statues of Sam Houston and Stephen F. Austin that were to be placed in the state building at the Exposition was meager, Miss Ney saw in it an opportunity for beginning her career once more.

After beginning her work in the basement of the Capitol, Miss Ney saw that the commission could open the opportunity for beginning her career once more, and she determined to open a studio in Hyde Park, a suburb of Austin. Her working place would be Formosa, named for the studio in Madeira, and construction was begun in 1892. Austin, at the time, was certainly no center for art, and many of the resources and even tools necessary for a sculptor's work were not available. At one point, she expressed a "desire to get one of Galveston Medical School's 'skelettons' for a while . . . I had for my first statue the use of the Blind Asylum skeleton, which I had to return."

The statue of Stephen F. Austin was not ready in time for the Chicago Exposition, but that of Sam Houston was. And it created so much interest that organizers tried in vain to persuade the Texans to allow it to be moved to the central building of the exposition. Certainly both members of the committee and Miss Ney were disappointed that only one of the two Texans was represented. But once more personal affairs had interfered with Miss Ney's work. Son Lorne had returned to Texas, and former Governor Roberts was now at the new University of Texas law department. Plans were made for Lorne to attend the University under the watchful eye of his parents' friend. Although the beginning was propitious, he quickly lost interest and by the time of the Exposition he had returned to Liendo and eloped with the sixteen-year-old daughter of a former county judge of Waller County.

With Miss Ney in Austin, the duties of running what had grown to be a 2,200-acre plantation fell to her husband. In writing about Montgomery, Stephens calls the period from 1873 to 1893 the most productive of the philosopher's life, but the departure of Elisabet made it essential that he face the realities of the plantation. During this time, Dr. Montgomery became interested in political philosophy, a fact that is reflected in his writing. On a more practical level he became interested in local government and served as county commissioner for Waller County for two terms from 1895 to 1899.

Thus in the third decade of their residence in Texas, Miss Ney was making a place for herself in the state. So, also, was Dr. Montgomery. Several factors probably combined to bring this about. Dr. Montgomery obtained a copy of their marriage certificate from Madeira about the time he obtained United States citizenship in 1884. Since a wife acquired the citizenship of her husband, it is probable that he made known its existence to the authorities. Thus were laid to rest questions about the matrimonial status of the pair. Second, in speeches made in Hempstead, Dr. Montgomery expressed ideas that were interesting and informative to his audience. At the same time, he was apparently deeply interested in the development of Prairie View Normal and Industrial School, which was established on the plantation adjoining Liendo. After his wife's move to Austin, he helped organize the Texas Academy of Science and served as its president.

In Austin, residents may have first been impressed by the presence of a renowned sculptor in their midst. After the completion of the statues of Stephen F. Austin and Sam Houston as well as busts of such men as Oran M. Roberts, John H. Reagan, Francis R. Lubbock, Sir Swante Palm, William Jennings Bryan, Joseph D. Sayers, and others, they were assured that Miss Ney was a working artist. Although there were several painters of some reputation in the city and there was an appreciation of music, sculpture was generally an unfamiliar art.

Throughout her life Elisabet Ney was an individual and had a flair for the dramatic. In Austin, her clothing became the object of considerable comment, although most women sculptors wore a similar costume during that time. Photographs of American sculptor Harriet Hosmer (1830-1908) show her wearing studio clothes almost identical to those worn by Miss Ney. Bride Neill Taylor gave the following description of Miss Ney's dress:

> If visitors to the studio arrived during the artist's working hours, they found her garbed in a black velvet tunic that came but little below the knees. It is true that — even in the hottest weather — close buttoned leggings of serge, sometimes black, sometimes gray, endeavored to supply whatever modesty, at that day, seemed to demand in atonement for such radical abbreviation of skirts. But no Texan had ever before seen a mature woman in a garment that stopped short of her feet — most dresses trailed in the dust — and the shock was severe. During her hours of leisure, they found the artist in garments long enough, and full enough, and conventionally modest enough — but still different, and, therefore, reprehensible. In public she wore a gray silk cloak, that covered her completely, and a little black velvet close-fitting headpiece draped with a veil of rare lace which, though fit and unobtrusive enough — was also different, and so again made her the object of disapproving notice wherever she went.

Miss Ney in turn felt that women of the day uncomfortably dressed were "clothed against every law of beauty, freedom and comfort." When friends attempted to call attention to Miss Ney's abilities, people usually asked, "Why doesn't she dress like other women?"

A few Austin residents recall Miss Ney and Mr. Ralph Bickler, who knew her as "Tante" (Aunt) Ney, remembers:

> . . . Mother invited her to supper frequently and served homemade rye bread and cottage cheese with rich cream over it. Miss Ney often brought some watercress from the spring-fed creek at the rear of her studio and that was enjoyed along with the cottage cheese.
>
> On one of these occasions, I went into the backyard and dug up a lump of mud and fashioned it into the shape and size of a corncob. I took an old corncob and pressed it against my mud 'creation' which made it appear more real. I took it in and showed it to Miss Ney. She complimented me, patted me on the head and instructed me to 'keep on trying.
>
> One happy recollection is of an Easter egg hunt at Formosa, her studio home in Hyde Park. Miss Ney had brought dozens of eggs to Mother's home to be colored and prepared for the hunt. Other friends were called upon also to prepare eggs. That Easter we went out to Miss

> Ney's along with many friends and their children. At a given signal, the children were told to find the eggs that the Easter Rabbit had hidden. We swarmed over the grounds and it happened that I found more eggs than any other child. My reward came later.
>
> Miss Ney was of a romantic nature and had planned an unusual event. On the back side of her estate, Miss Ney had a small, private lake that she had created by having a stone dam built across the small spring-fed creek. For this occasion, Signor Docchi, an Italian stonecutter who worked for Miss Ney and assisted her as well in other ways, transformed a flat-bottomed wooden rowboat into a gondola. It was indeed a transformation. It had a graceful prow and a colorful canopy was placed at the rear of the gondola. Miss Ney had invited two young ladies to take a ride in the gondola. Dixie and Marie Graham were the first and only ladies to go for a gondola ride. The ladies took seats under the canopy and the gondolier, dressed in an immaculate white uniform, 'poled' the gondola up and down the 'lake' a couple of times. Then he brought the gondola to the landing for a christening ceremony. My reward, as mentioned above, was to break a bottle of champagne on the gondola's prow. Just at that moment, a strong gust of wind caught the canopy and it appeared that the gondola would be turned on its side. The gondolier stuck his pole into the mud and my big brother Harry entered the water to 'rescue' the ladies. He helped them ashore amid a round of applause. No damage was done, except to Harry's trousers. He had sunk knee-deep in the mud. Next, the mud was washed from his trousers with a stream of water from the garden hose, but Harry was still in a predicament. He had to go into the studio for a change of trousers. Miss Ney had none for him, but she loaned him a robe to wear while his trousers got a quick drying treatment of some kind. Nevertheless, the whole affair was a great success and was thoroughly enjoyed by all of those who were present.
>
> The prize or reward mentioned previously for finding the most Easter eggs was the privilege or honor of breaking a bottle of champagne on the prow of the gondola in the christening ceremony. A strong piece of twine was tied to a tree branch overhanging the gondola and then tied to the neck of the bottle. At a given signal, I released the bottle and it swung through the air and broke against the gondola. Great applause followed the event.

Miss Ney never moved her official residence to Austin; her home was always in Hempstead. She only came to Austin to work.

In 1895, Miss Ney decided to return unannounced to Germany for a visit. Not only was there the satisfaction about her work in Texas but also she had discovered that the studio that Ludwig II had given her was just as she left it. Although she had been gone for a quarter of a century, she was received enthusiastically in Berlin and Munich. After selling the studio in Munich to secure funds for Formosa and shipping some of her works to Austin, she, herself, returned to Texas. She visited in Europe again in 1902 and 1903.

The sculptress gained considerable recognition on January 19, 1903, when in the State Capitol, statues of her works of Austin and Houston were unveiled with appropriate ceremony. Earlier replicas had been unveiled in the National Capitol in Washington. In addition, the Texas Division of the United Daughters of the Confederacy undertook a project in 1902 to secure funds for a memorial to be placed over the grave of General Albert Sidney Johnston in the State Cemetery. Many critics consider the Johnston work among her best. It was also during this time that she began her ideal figure of Lady Macbeth. One of her last pieces was executed in 1905 for the grave of Mrs. Emma Schnerr in Fredericksburg. During these years she was a great stimulus to artistic appreciation in the state. She organized the Texas Academy of Fine Arts and promoted the instruction of art in the public schools and at the University of Texas. She lobbyed for legislative support of art in public buildings. Her efforts in all these areas led to activities that culminated in the formation of the Texas Fine Arts Association.

Early in 1907 Miss Ney's health began to fail. She developed heart trouble complicated by bronchial problems that resulted from the marble dust attendant to completion of work on the Albert Sidney Johnston piece. Her husband came to stay with her and was with her when she died at her studio on January 19, 1907. Her body was taken back to Liendo and placed under a grove of live oak trees she and Dr. Montgomery had planted more than thirty years before.

Elisabet Ney and Edmund Montgomery had a long and devoted marriage as attested by their mutual admiration and respect for each other. When apart, they wrote often. Perhaps her views on marriage were unusual for that day but they were understood by her husband. And he was a man of strength who helped shape her ideas as no one else. If he appeared sometimes to be dominated by his wife, this situation could be explained by the circumstances of his own work and interests in which he was so involved.

Dr. Montgomery continued to live at Liendo, his health declining steadily until his death on April 17, 1911. He was also buried at Liendo, the ashes of his son Arthur having been placed in his coffin. Their son Lorne died in 1913 after an injury resulting either from a fall from a horse or a balcony. Perhaps because his service in the Spanish American War had brought considerable pride to himself as well as to his parents, he asked that he be buried at Arlington National Cemetery.

Like many artists Elisabet Ney suffered over money matters. And the viewer of her works is saddened by the thought that the years of inactivity she spent at Liendo were prime years that could have been spent in some kind of artistic productivity. Her biographer, recalling the time when Miss Ney arrived at Liendo and predicted that she would live and die there made this comment: "Texas gained much that day, but Elisabet Ney lost. No one who knew the intimate details of her life can fail to realize that the enrichment of Texas was at the expense to the artist of bitter heart sorrows and an obstructed hindered career."

Nevertheless, working under difficult — even primitive — conditions and plagued with personal sorrows, she created works that brought her international renown. And to Texas she has a special significance, for she was the first internationally acclaimed artist to live and work in the Lone Star State. In a very real sense, her arrival in Austin marked the birth of serious art in Texas.

# Mollie Bailey

MOLLIE BAILEY

# Mollie Bailey

## "THE CIRCUS QUEEN ON THE SOUTHWEST"

by
HAROLD B. SIMPSON

It was cotton picking time down in Texas

And the leaves of all the trees a golden brown.

The children and the old folks were happy

For the Mollie Bailey show had come to town.

Mollie Bailey was perhaps the best known and most beloved woman in Texas at the time of her death in 1918. To use an old cliche — she was a legend in her time. Today, however, except for those persons born before the turn of the century, her name is relatively unknown and her circus all but forgotten. Her fame passed with that of the boys in gray, whose cause she espoused and whose hearts she had captured. "Aunt Mollie," as she was affectionately known by her thousands of friends throughout Texas, has been described by those who knew her best as a woman of "great charm," whose "eternal spirit of youth [and] integrity . . . endeared her to people." Mrs. Irene Pipkin of Waco once described her as "pretty, quick-witted, and altogether charming in manner." She was "a cultured woman" Mrs. Pipkin added, "always poised, always using good English and never resorting to slang of any kind." Another acquaintance wrote that "she always wore beautiful clothes and her diamonds were large and beautiful, and her smile, her dark eyes seemed to glisten as her jewelry." And yet another friend remarked that Mollie Bailey "believed that laughter and happiness were necessary for the health of humanity. She took pride in bringing pleasure to people . . . . Her primary aim seemed to make people happy; her secondary aim to make money." According to a life long associate, Mollie Bailey had a realistic philosophy of life, "We cannot take it with us," she often remarked, "Do some good as you go along and leave a good name with the people you have met. I don't want the earth, and some day, I shall get only a small space in it." Mollie had a favorite verse which read, "If all the love that's left unsaid were broadcast here and there, there would not be a hungry heart, nor yet a single tear."

The Circus Queen of the Southwest was born Mollie Arline Kirkland on November 2, 1844, at a plantation near Mobile, Alabama. Her father, William Kirkland, was a prominant planter of Irish-English ancestry, and her mother, Mary, was a French beauty. Kirkland was a relatively large slave owner and his cotton fields covered hundreds of acres of rich Sumter County bottomland. Mollie grew up in this "Gone With the Wind" setting and she remained a true daughter of the Old South all of her life.

Somewhat of a tomboy as a girl, Mollie matured into a beautiful young lady. While attending a female academy near Tuscaloosa, Alabama, she was chosen as one of the most beautiful girls in the state. It was while attending the Alabama girl's school that her talent for acting and dancing was first recognized. The headmistress wrote to William Kirkland commending his daughter for her outstanding work in the fields of "dramatics and tableaux."

When Mollie came home for the summer, after her year at the boarding school, she saw her first circus. Although forbidden by her father to attend the traveling show, she stole away to nearby Mobile and watched the performance. Little did Mollie realize at the time that she was viewing a form of entertainment that would drastically change her life. It was to provide her with both a livelihood and a husband.

As Mollie, wide-eyed and excited, viewed the panorama that was enfolding under the big top, her attention was soon fixed on the red-headed cornet player, the leader of the circus band. The young musician was James Augustus Bailey, the son of the circus owner. "Gus" Bailey, a very talented musician and a distant relative of the Bailey of later Barnum & Bailey fame, returned the affectionate glances. It apparently was love at first sight for both of them. They met secretly, exchanged vows of fidelity, and made plans to get married. Only one major barrier stood in the way of their plans, but it was a formidable one — the six foot and three inch, 300 pound William Kirkland. Although Mollie had secured her Gaelic mother's permission, her father was appalled by his fourteen year old daughter's intentions. Nothing could convince the Southern planter that his well-bred and beautiful teen age daughter should marry the twenty-four year old itinerate musician and circus performer. Mollie, upset, but undeterred by her father's objection to the marriage, with her mother's blessing left home one day when her father had gone to Mobile on business, met Gus, and they were married on March 21, 1858.

Mollie never saw her father again. Although she returned home twice to ask his forgiveness, he refused to talk or even to see her. Kirkland, left destitute by the war, his wife in failing health, brooded his life away, his heart broken by his favorite daughter. Mollie wrote to him after her mother's death, but the letters were never answered. Even naming one of her sons, William Kirkland Bailey, had no effect on the old patriarch. A few years after the war, she learned through relatives of her father's death. But now she had no desire to visit her early plantation home, which, she understood, had fallen into decay from the lack of attention.

Mollie and Gus spent their honeymoon traveling with his father's circus, but soon made plans to organize a show of their own. Gus' brother, Alfred, and Mollie's half-sister, Sally, joined the young couple in their new enterprise. Several additional performers were hired and the "Bailey Family Troupe" — more of a vaudeville show than a circus, started on the entertainment circuit. Playing in small town school auditoriums and opera houses across the South from the Carolinas to Arkansas, the Bailey show was a success from the start. Mollie was the leading lady, the soloist and the organist. Gus, the leading man in the saccharin dramas that were staged as part of the show, played the fiddle as the leader of the small orchestra, and was the troupe's top comedian. Alfred also wore more than one hat, he was billed as a contortionist and played in the band, while Sally performed in the one-act melodramas and danced. Mollie's first child was born while on the circuit in Arkansas.

With the coming of the Civil War, the show disbanded. Gus enlisted in the Forty-fourth Alabama Infantry at Selma, Alabama, on May 20, 1861, but in the winter of 1862-63 he transferred to Company B of the Third Arkansas Infantry, a regiment in Hood's Texas Brigade. He soon became leader of the Third Arkansas Band and performed with the "Hood's Minstrels" — a group of talented actors, musicians and singers who were members of the famous Brigade. Gus helped to write the rollicking marching song of the Brigade that has endured several wars — " The Old Grey Mare." Mollie, in the meantime, did her bit for the Confederacy. She nursed the sick and wounded, smuggled medicine through the lines, and, as she herself admitted, "occasionally acted as a spy." Disguised as an old lady peddling pies, she strolled through Federal camps several times bringing back valuable information. Mollie and her sister Sally during the winter months, while the Brigade was in semi-permanent quarters, joined the Hood's Minstrels in entertaining the troops with their song and dance acts. A soldier in attendance at the winter quarters entertainment noted that the "performers, each and all, deserve the thanks of their fellow-soldiers; and especially Mrs. Bailey, who, by her fine acting and vocal powers, elevated the whole affair to the rank of a first class entertainment." Gus, never a very robust figure, was physically drained by the war and as time passed would come to depend more and more upon Mollie to "carry on the show" and provide the livelihood for the family. The war taught Mollie to appreciate the valor and steadfastness of the Confederate soldier and to appreciate his dedication to duty as he saw it. Consequently, Confederate veterans and their immediate families never had to pay to see a Mollie Bailey Show.

Following Appomattox, the Baileys' returned to the "land of the razorbacks" with the remnants of his regiment. Now with three daughters to feed, two children being born during the war, they had little time to dwell upon the defeat of the South. Earning a living being paramount, Mollie and Gus signed on with a theatrical company plying the Mississippi on a stern-wheel steamer. At first this life appealed to the young song and dance team. As a matter of fact, within a year they organized their own company, paid down on a sidewheeler, and presented the most popular melodramas of the day, Edna Ferber style, to the townspeople along the Lower Mississippi. Mollie now realized one of her early ambitions — real dramatic acting. The company's favorite play was one of the traditionals, "All is Not Gold That Glitters." After two years of "showboating", however, the Baileys realized that a Mississippi steamer was no place to bring up a family. To Mollie, her family always came first, Gus and the children were the most important things in her life. So in 1869, the Bailey's traded their interest in the showboat to a Mississippi planter for money and a team of mules and a wagon to make the long awaited trip to Texas.

Ever since Gus had served along side Texas troops during the war, the couple had talked of settling in the Lone Star State. Now, leaving the graves of two of their young daughters, Dixie and Ada, behind in Mississippi, Gus and Mollie and the remaining children with a wagon load of costumes, instruments and props started their mule team west. The Baileys, who now called their aggregation the "Bailey Concert Company," got only as far as Arkansas. Here they set up headquarters at the town of Prescott and played towns in southern Arkansas and Northeast Texas for the next several years.

The Arkansas years were happy ones for the Baileys. Their Concert Company gave performances in schoolhouses in the rural areas and in small towns. Mollie played the little portable organ, Gus played the fiddle and another member of the company played the drums. The children, though small, sang and did a few dance acts. The Bailey Concert Company was a successful venture. Mollie, however, to help meet expenses during the winters spent at Prescott, operated a dancing school in the village opera house. She taught dancing every winter while they were in Arkansas, taking time out occasionally to give birth to another child. In all, Mollie and Gus had nine children. Naming the birth places of their offspring sounded like a roll call of the Southern states. Mississippi, Alabama, Missouri, North Carolina, Arkansas and Texas were claimed as native states by the Bailey children.

The Bailey Circus was born during the winter of 1879-80, when Mollie and Gus decided to expand the Concert Company into a wagon circus and leave Arkansas for permanent residence in Texas. A train of circus wagons, tents and other paraphernalia were quickly assembled and, what was soon to be billed as, "A Texas Show for Texas People," moved across the Red River.

The circus was complete even to the flags that fluttered from the center pole of the big top. The Baileys considered themselves Texans since serving with Hood's Brigade even though they did not permanently settle in the State until 1880. Mollie, to show her allegiance to Texas, had flown the Bonnie Blue flag along with the Confederate flag at all of their performances on both land and water after the war. In 1880 they added the Stars and Stripes and all three flags were then flown at each performance from that year on.

Circuses had ventured south of the Red River and west of the Sabine before Mollie and Gus made their appearance. According to G.G. Sturtevant, the circus was probably the first form of professional entertainment to visit the Lone Star State and its appeal was instant. The first such entertainment that came to Texas was John Robinson's Great Southern Show. The year was 1850, and Robinson's extravaganza proved such a financial success that it attracted other such shows and circuses to the State. The next show of merit to play in Texas was Mabie's Circus and Menagerie which crossed the Sabine from Louisiana in 1858. Mabie was reputed to have had the best menagerie in the United States. Included among his animals were three very large elephants, the largest of which was "Romeo," a huge male valued at $30,000. The bull pachyderm was almost lost, however, when he fell through a wooden bridge near Waco. Orton and Older's Circus visited the State in 1859, and introducted the Negro Minstrel Show to the Southwest. It was the last circus to play in Texas until after the war. In late 1865, the United States Circus owned by Haight and Chambers, which traveled by boat from New Orleans, played before large crowds at Galveston. During the 1870's two nationally known shows came through the State. Dan Rice, the famous clown, brought his circus to Texas in the early part of that decade, and Charles W. Noyes, who owned the Crescent City Circus, came in later by ship via the Red River from Alexandria, Louisiana. Then came the Bailey Circus in the 1880's. It was destined for a long run in the Lone Star State — over forty years of *continuous* operation from 1880 to the early 1920's.

Mollie and Gus called two Texas cities and one Texas town home during the years that the circus operated in the State. Their first headquarters was in Dallas. Here they owned a home at the corner of South Preston and Young Streets. In the late 1880's, Mollie purchased a large lot and a house in Blum, and in 1890 the Bailey's moved their home and circus headquarters to this small community in the northwest corner of Hill County. Their home in Blum was located above Schoolhouse Creek, a small stream that meanders through the outskirts of the community. In the mid-1890's, the Baileys made their last move, this time to Houston. They owned a half block of land in the Bayou City between Dunbar and Oak streets. On this site their home was built — four adjoining cottages. They also owned a small ranch a mile out of town that was used principally for entertaining their many friends and for recreational week-ends. The circus was housed and quartered during the winter months in Texas at these three locations.

Gus, who had been in failing health for a number of years, never traveled with the circus again after they moved to Blum. With his retirement from the road, the show became officially known as the "Mollie A. Bailey Show" — a name that the country people had called the circus for years. When Gus died at Houston in June 1896, Mollie shouldered the complete administrative and financial burden of the growing enterprise — a management task of great responsibility. She now became and remained the only woman in the world known to have owned and successfully operated a circus.

After moving to Blum, the Bailey Circus entered its "Golden Age." Although still basically a family endeavor, other performers were hired, the number of wagons was increased, new tents were purchased and several animals were added to the menagerie. The show could now boast of thirty-one wagons, 170 head of stock, twenty-one trained ponies and a motley collection of walking animals. The main tent had tiered seats on three sides and a curtained stage on the fourth, with a large ring in the center. Several smaller tents flanked the big top, including a mess tent, one that housed the menagerie, and another in which side shows were featured.

By 1890, three of the nine children born to Gus and Mollie had died, but the remaining six talented offspring under their father's and mother's guidance and training contributed greatly to the success of the show. Eugene managed the waltzing, ball-playing, precision drilled "educated ponies" and also doubled as a musician and clown. Son Allie handled the "trained canines", played the trombone, and performed on the fallaway ladder and slack-wire. Willie (William Kirkland Bailey) helped his mother with business details and played the cornet in the circus band. Brad, the youngest son, did a tumbling act and walked on the high wire, while daughters Minnie sang and Birda showed her "human canaries" and performed her "floating serpentine dance." These family acts were supplemented by professional contortionists, clowns and musicians. Mollie herself handled ticket sales, most of the promotional endeavors, the purchasing of equipment and supplies, and the payroll which numbered some sixty employees.

By the turn of the century the Mollie A. Bailey Show was the most sought after entertainment in the state. "County fairs waited for it; Confederate veterans dated their reunions with its appearance; it was in demand!" Several days before her show was scheduled to appear at a particular town, families would start arriving and camp out near the show grounds to watch the wagons roll in, the parade of the animals and the raising of the big top. One of the reasons for the great popularity of Mollie's Circus was that it provided good, clean entertainment in an era when many fake and shoddy shows were traveling through the country. In fact, many towns would permit only her show to play their community.

Mollie did not use an advance agent until her show "went on the rails," and then the agent's job was largely confined to carrying out her specific instructions. In the 1890's and early 1900's she personally promoted her circus and was a master at human relations and mass psychology. When the circus was scheduled into a town in which it had never played before she generally played a double stand. Townspeople were admitted free to the first performance just to get acquainted. A few of the acts were changed and the great majority of those who attended the opening show then paid to see the second show. The next time that she played that community she could be almost certain of a full house. Often times Mollie would announce that all or a certain percentage of the proceeds from a particular performance would be turned over to charity or contributed to a local church or Confederate monument building fund. It has been said that her contributions have been largely responsible for the building of at least fifty churches in Texas and scores of Confederate memorials and monuments. She bought the expendable supplies and food needed by the circus from local merchants where she happened to be playing, and she did all of the shopping personally so as to be able to meet as many people in the town as possible. Too, it was her custom to stand at the main entrance to the big top and to personally welcome everyone who entered. Her friendliness and great human qualities earned her the name "Aunt Mollie" — an affectionate sobriquet that she relished. Her advertising broadsides were simple, they made no extravagent claims of "ferocious animals," "unusual freaks" and "death-defying acts." They changed little from year to year as can be seen by looking through the Hertzberg Collection of Circusana in the San Antonio Public Library, where much memorabilia of the Mollie A. Bailey Show is maintained. Practically all of her advance handbills were headlined with the simple expression, "Aunt Mollie's Coming" — that is all that she needed to say to create interest in her visit.

In an effort to identify herself and her troupe directly with the communities in which they played and to be sure of a good central location for the circus, Mollie purchased scores of lots in small towns throughout Texas. It has been estimated that at one time she owned as many as 150 lots. When the circus was not using the space (which was all but one or two days a year) she permitted the ground to be used for local community activities such as church socials, baseball games, band concerts, etc. When the circus converted from wagons to railroad cars fro transportation in 1904, it was no longer possible to visit many of her old stops — those towns that were not located on or near a railroad. Thus, many of the lots were no longer needed, and in most of these cases Mollie deeded the property to the community or let it go for taxes. At her death, however, she still owned about fifty circus lots in various parts of the state.

The Old South and the Confederate veteran occupied a special niche in Mollie's heart. Having been born and raised on a Mississippi plantation, being directly involved in the war, and married to a Confederate veteran, she was a true daughter of Dixie. She was so imbued with the cause and spirit of the South that she named a daughter born during the war after Dan Decatur Emmett's famous minstrel and Confederate marching song, "Dixie." Following the war, as noted previously, she and Gus kept alive the old states rights spirit of the South by flying both the Bonnie Blue and the Confederate battle flags during their performances. And all that a man who had worn the Gray had to do, was to identify himself for free admittance to a Bailey show. When the Baileys moved permanently to Texas, this privilege was later extended to all Civil War veterans, Northern as well as Southern.

J. Marvin Hunter, Sr., the late distinguished editor and publisher of *Frontier Times,* remembered the Mollie A. Bailey Circus well, having watched the show as a small boy both at Menardville and at Mason. Over the years the Hunter and Bailey families became close friends and young J. Marvin came to know Aunt Mollie quite well. In later years he recalled an incident that happened in 1892, which was characteristic of the Circus Queen's generosity and her deep attachment for the Confederate Veteran. Marvin Hunter's father was editor and owner of the Mason *Herald* at the time and Mollie Bailey had just arrived in town with her show. According to Hunter,

> Aunt Mollie sent for [his] father to come to the show grounds on the public square. As soon as she greeted him cordially she said: "Mr. Hunter, are there any old Confederate soldiers here?" "Sure", said [his] father, "the woods are full of them." "Well, here's a bunch of reserve seat tickets, and I will ask you to pass them out to the old Confederate soldiers of this Community, and tell them their old friend, Mollie Bailey wants them to come to her show. And here, also are a few tickets to give to such orphan children as you may know here."

"That was Mollie Bailey's way," wrote the editor of the *Frontier Times*, and added, "once you met her and got acquainted she never forgot you and you didn't forget her."

Too, Mollie, was loyal to and sympathetic toward the Southern Negro. Those that she employed she treated as members of her family and took their part as she would that of her own children. She was partially raised by a "Southern Mammy" named Pansy, and her favorite playmates were Pansy's two small children, Alexander and Alice. Often in her later years, Mollie would reminisce about her early life on the plantation and her fondness for Pansy and her children. While living at Prescott, Arkansas, Mollie hired a Negro widow, Easter Roberts, to help take care of the numerous little

Baileys. Easter practically became a member of the family and one of her sons, Will, traveled with the show. After the Bailey children had grown up, she left Mollie's employment and moved her family to Big Sandy, Texas. Easter and her children were always admitted to the Circus free when it was playing in their neighborhood. According to an article written about Aunt Mollie by her friend, Miss Vivian Richardson, which appeared in the Dallas *Morning News* during the summer of 1920,

> To the day of her death, Mollie's intense Southern loyalty burned brightly, and since in the clarity of her mind, precept was never divorced from deed, she was always paying some broken down Negro's way back to 'Jawgie' or giving one a bit of work.

Mollie would not hesitate to rally to the aid of a black employee when the occasion called for it. There were several towns in West Texas at that time that would not allow a Negro to live or to even remain within the corporate limits for an hour or two. Mollie had scheduled her circus into one such town soon after the show had taken to the rails. The word had preceded her coming that she had a Negro with her troupe. When the cars of the circus were switched onto the side track at that particular town in preparation to start unloading, the town constable came to see Mollie. He demanded that her Negro cook, Fred, leave immediately. Now occurred one of the few times that anyone can remember of Aunt Mollie getting her "Irish up." She told the officer that Fred was a part of her troupe and that his services were indispensable as he had the responsibility for feeding some 100 people. "You and your law makers are narrow, ignorant and mean," she exclaimed, and added, "I'll move the show on to the next town and lose this night. I'd rather not show anyway after this insult." Mollie then ordered the town constable off of her train, told him "never to speak to [her] again" and that if she "were [his] size [she'd] throw [him] out." The whole troupe came to her support, and vowed that they would leave the town without unloading, lose a day's wages, and boycott the town ever after. After talking it over, however, they decided they had a moral obligation to play the town as scores of people had traveled many miles by wagon to see the well advertised show and it would be unfair to let them down. Consequently, Fred was consulted and agreed to go on to the next town; the circus went on as scheduled but Mollie never played that community again.

As the years went by the circus expanded greatly. It grew from a score of performers and workers when the show first came to Texas in the early 1880's to a payroll of 100 by the late 1890's. Numerous acts were added with the employment of professional aerial artists, musicians, trick riders and animal handlers and trainers. By the early 1900's the menagerie had become quite respectable, consisting of camels, Indian elephants, bears, leopards and zebras in addition to a large number of animals native to the Southwest.

Once a groceryman in a small town asked Aunt Mollie when she was going to add a lion to her circus. She quickly replied, "Whenever I start charging a dollar for my show." She never increased the price of tickets to the circus during the forty years that her show operated in Texas — thirty-five cents for adults, twenty-five cents for children and ten cents for reserved seats. Too, Mollie was very liberal with free passes to war veterans and orphans, and gave families a special group rate.

Prior to the show being transported by rail in 1906, the larger animals posed a serious transportation problem. This dilemna was solved by having them walk from town to town behind the wagon train. Travelers coming upon this strange entourage ambling through the rural sections of Texas, were of course, quite startled. Horses and mules were particularly sensitive to the sight and smell of camels and elephants and many a thrown horseman and runaway team could charge his predicament to Mollie Bailey's pachyderms and dromendaries.

The elephants during their cross-country treks provided a number of amusing incidents. Clint Woods of Mabank, Texas, told of one. According to Woods, he was traveling one day in his Model T Ford through the red clay hills of East Texas after a heavy rain when he attempted to pass the Bailey animal train. The slick road had quite a crown to it and his car slid off into a ditch and stuck fast in the mud. Eugene Bailey, who had charge of the animals, agreed to let one of the larger elephants push Wood's car out of the ditch. This good Samaritan act almost cost the circus an elephant, for when the pachyderm placed his head against the Model T to push, Woods stepped on the gas and the exhaust fumes almost asphyxiated the beast. Groggy from the carbon monoxide, the elephant backed up and sat in the mud stupified. Woods' car was finally pulled out of the mud by a local farmer's team of horses. On another occasion, C.B. Allen of Ennis, Texas, was driving his new car near Cristoval in West Texas following the circus into town when his Ford developed motor trouble. Eugene, as usual, offered the services of his big bull, Jimmie. Allen accepted, and Jimmie placed his head against the back of the car and pushed it all the way into town. To the car owner's surprise, he found that Jimmie had left a souvenir of his efforts — the print of his head in the back of the vehicle where he had noticably "pushed the metal in."

October 2, 1906, was an eventful day for Mollie Bailey. This was the day that "A Texas Show for Texas People," which had traveled by wagons since its inception, was going to make the switch to railroad cars. At Garland, Texas, on this fall day in 1906 the Circus Queen of the Southwest took delivery of three cars — a Pullman and two freight cars of the Arms Palace type. The Pullman included private staterooms, a large dining room and a well appointed kitchen. The freight cars housed the animals, equipment, tents and other circus paraphernalia. These cars would remain the home of the circus for the last fifteen years of its existence. Aunt Mollie enjoyed the convenience, luxury and speed of railroad travel but she missed the picturesque trips through the Texas countryside and visiting with her friends in the small towns that now had to be by-passed. Too, there would be no more elephants pushing Model T Fords out of Texas mud and along Texas byways. One era has passed and another one was at hand.

At each stop now Mollie held open house in the Pullman. No sooner would the three cars be pulled off on the siding when she would be on the back platform welcoming her friends aboard. It would be one big party with Mollie Bailey as hostess until the circus cars moved on to the next stop, and then the proceedings would start all over again. As a matter of fact, a saying was coined by Colonel Davenport, a well-known editorial writer of the day, that described Mollie's socializing from town to town. Davenport referred to persons who traveled about and entertained constantly as "Just Mollie Baileying around." The phrase caught on and became a well-known national expression before World War I.

Mr. E. E. Hayes, eighty-nine years young, who grew up in Montgomery County, Texas, but is now a resident of Longview, Washington, well remembered Mollie and her circus. In a letter to the author, Hayes stated,

> I knew Mollie Bailey when she was operating her show in East Texas in 1910 and a few years later, and remember that almost all the people in Montgomery County knew her as "Aunt Mollie." She knew scores of people by first names, and at each stop she sat upon a thronelike chair and held a sort of royal reception. It was "Howdy, Ebby, Howdy, Jim," and "My goodness, how little Jimmy has grown!" Her equipment was always bright and shiney and the costumes did not have the threadbare look of small shows in East Texas of those days.

Not all of the Pullman car visitors were ordinary folks from the rural areas. Many of the most famous men of Texas chatted over coffee in the cars with Aunt Mollie. Senators Joe Bailey and Morris Sheppard and Governors O. B. Colquitt and James Hogg seldom failed to pay her a visit when the circus train was in their vicinity. Some of her best friends and honored guests though were men that she had known during the war as officers in Hood's Texas Brigade. Numbered among these were Major E. K. Goree and Captains James Hunter and W. H. Gaston. Mollie especially enjoyed these reunions with Hood's lieutenants and together they relived the old camp days in Tennessee and Virginia and talked of her beloved Gus.

All was not moonlight and roses for Mollie and her troupe. Indians, cyclones, tornados, and a murder scare gave some anxious moments, but fortunately the "perils of Pauline" — Mollie in this case — were successfully weathered with no harm done. In the early 1870's, when the show was working out of Prescott, Arkansas, and playing engagements in the frontier towns of Texas, it was visited by a party of unfriendly Indians. On this particular occasion the circus was traveling between two settlements, and had stopped out on the prairie for the night. The wagons were arranged in a circle as usual, and Mollie was in the act of preparing supper for Gus and the children when the cry "Indians" was heard. The children were herded into the wagons and the adults scattered about looking for anything that could be used for a weapon. Mollie ran to a trunk in her wagon and took out the pistol that she had carried since the Civil War. She fired several shots in the air but the Indians could not be scared off and kept advancing in an ever decreasing circle toward the wagon train. Suddenly she thought of the big circus drum in one of the wagons, hastily uncovering it, she commenced to beat the bass drum furiously. The warriors, awed and frightened by what they thought to be artillery, "wheeled their horses, and fled in terror, not even pausing to look back." Indians had little fear of the pop of small arms fire, but it was a well known fact that they feared the boom of the white man's artillery or "thunder wagons", their name for cannons. Mollie related this incident many years later to the famous Comanche chief, Quanah Parker, who thought it quite a joke. He never tired of hearing the tale and always requested Mollie to repeat it whenever they met.

Cyclones and tornados hit near the show on several occasions, but fortunately caused little damage to equipment and no injuries among the circus personnel. The first violent storm that struck where the circus was playing occurred at Lamesa in 1907. Near dusk, after the show, a funnel cloud was sighted and the performers scattered to storm cellars in town. The train was spared and little damage was done in town but all had received a good scare. In the following years cyclones and tornados hit near the circus while it was playing at Snyder, Oklahoma, and Nocona and Sherman, Texas. Straws were driven into trees, boulders were hurled through the air like pebbles and huge trees were uprooted but the Mollie A. Bailey Circus remained unscathed. The tornado that struck Sherman hit about the same time that the circus arrived in town and it was a particularly devastating one. According to eye witness accounts of the Sherman storm,

> A splinter was driven through six cans of concentrated lye . . . . A dead snake was wrapped several times around the limb of a surviving tree. A trunk top was found 35 miles north of Sherman, the name of the owner still readable on it. A cabinet phonograph was picked up twenty miles from where it belonged. A doctor who was driving along on his way to make a call, was caught up, whirled in the storm, and deposited later minus his clothes. The next day a friend brought a wheel of his buggy

to him, all that was ever found of the vehicle. His horse was found half a mile away stripped of his harness. A rural school teacher was picked up 35 miles north of his school.

One night, in 1913, when playing an engagement at a small town in Southeastern Texas and after most of the personnel had retired for the evening, several shots rang out near the circus grounds. Eugene, who was playing dominoes with his wife, stepped out of the train to investigate the cause of the disturbance. As he drew near to the area from which he thought the shots came he was seized by an armed mob of local townspeople bent on giving someone a "necktie party." As Eugene was being dragged toward the hanging tree his coat was ripped open and the Odd Fellows emblem on his watch fob was exposed. The leader of the mob, seeing the fraternal fob and being a member of the same organization called a halt to the proceedings and ordered Eugene to be released. It had been a case of mistaken identity. The son of a local bank president had been assaulted and nearly killed by a man with whom he was playing cards. Witnesses saw the man flee toward the circus cars and presumed that he belonged with the show. A posse was hastily organized, proceeded to the circus area clearing their guns on the way, and came across Eugene who was investigating the shooting. All's well that ends well but the affair gave Aunt Mollie and Eugene's wife a few anxious moments.

Undaunted by such violent acts of man and nature, the Bailey Circus continued to perform daily throughout Texas and Oklahoma ten months a year from February through November. Two months, December and January, were allowed for rest, recuperation, refurbishment and repair. The routing of the show from February 2 through March 18, 1913, not only provides an indication of the close scheduling adhered to, but gives a good cross section of the size of towns that it performed in.

| | | | | | |
|---|---|---|---|---|---|
| Feb. | 2 Humble | Feb. | 17 Cushing | March | 4 Warren |
| | 3 Shepherd | | 18 Nacagdoches | | 5 Saron |
| | 4 Livingston | | 19 Timpson | | 6 Groveton |
| | 5 Onalaska | | 20 Waterman | | 7 Benford |
| | 6 Trinity | | 21 Carthage | | 9 Corrigan |
| | 7 New Waverly | | 23 Center | | 10 Diboll |
| | 9 Conroe | | 24 Pineland | | 11 New Waverly |
| | 10 Fostoria | | 25 Jasper | | 12 Humble |
| | 11 Fuquay | | 26 Evadale | | 13 Cleveland |
| | 12 Saratoga | | 27 Silsbee | | 14 Montgomery |
| | 13 Kountze | | 28 Village Mills | | 16 Somerville |
| | 14 Doucette | March | 2 Woodville | | 17 Bellville |
| | 16 Huntington | | 3 Colmesneil | | 18 Sealy |

Many of the above towns could count only a few hundred residents and the largest had only a few thousand at most, but they were all located on or near the railroad and thus available for Mollie's road show. For obvious reasons, towns of this size never attracted the large national circuses and the Mollie Bailey Show was the only circus that many of the rural sections of Texas ever knew.

Although Aunt Mollie was in a profession that was not particularly noted for its high morals and clean living, particularly among the roustabouts, she herself was above reproach and saw to it that her performers and employees followed her high standards. She did not drink, smoke or use profane language or "even slang" — one of her best friends related. The smell of liquor on a man's breath would get him fired and profanity was not tolerated a second time. Research has not disclosed her church preference, but she lived a good Christian life and adhered religiously to the Ten Commandments and abided by the Golden Rule.

Although it is not generally known, Mollie introduced motion pictures to Texas. The "films" were one reelers, the mechanism crude and the accomodations uncomfortable, but they were a great drawing card. The "movies" were shown in a separate tent as a side show attraction. Her first reels consisted of an old-fashioned Fourth of July parade, a comic cavorting with a large fat hog, a sentimental love story, and, what was purported to be, the sinking of the battleship *USS Maine*. Each year a few new reels would be added. Thousands of Texans got their first glimpse of the Hollywood industry via Aunt Mollie's flickers.

The Circus Queen of the Southwest went into semi-retirement in 1914. She remained in Houston that year to care for her sick daughter, Birda, when the circus started its sweep north through East Texas. Although not physically with the show she continued to manage it by means of daily telegraph messages, detailed letters and telephone calls to her four sons. When Birda died in September 1917, it appeared to take something out of Aunt Mollie. Her friends noticed that she had lost some of her vitality and vivaciousness.

One early summer day in 1918, when Mollie was puttering around in her flower garden, she fell and broke her hip. At her advanced age, the break healed slowly and she languished in bed for several months. In late September her condition grew worse and the children in Houston summoned those outside of the city. She was taken by ambulance to St. Joseph's infirmary, where she lapsed into unconsciousness and remained in a coma for several days. Mollie A. Baily died on October 2, 1918, at Houston, just one month before her seventy-fourth birthday. The following touching eulogy of the Circus Queen appeared as the last paragraph in a biography written by her daughter-in-law, Olga Bailey, in 1943;

> And now, dear Aunt Mollie, we leave you. We know that you have signed up with a great company up there; that you are booked with such stars as Gus Bailey, Will Rogers, and others, who made the world a brighter place while they were in it. We know that the Great Director has found a place for you and that recognizing your worth, he will place you in a stellar role, as you deserve to be placed.

Aunt Mollie was not forgotten by the Circus lovers of Texas. When the Texas chapter of the Circus Fans Association of America was formed at Dallas in the 1920's, the Chapter was given the name of "Mollie A. Bailey Top." Paine L. Bush, former judge of the 68th District Court of Dallas, wrote,

> Almost all traces of the physical properties of the Mollie Bailey Circus have disappeared, but there remains something more durable than wood and stone, and that is the memory, which thousands of grateful Texans cherish, of the clean and wholesale entertainment which Mollie Bailey and her circus brought to Texas people . . . .

Mollie Bailey was a trail blazer in the entertainment field. Women like her deserve a special place in the history of the United States. Resolute and resourceful, persevering and proud, generous and gregarious, intelligent and talented, Mollie A. Bailey, a Texan by choice, was the prototype of American womanhood at its best. Texas was much richer for the many years that this remarkable lady and her family lived and performed in the State.

How we marveled at her diamonds,
So huge, so lustrous and bright.
But we never envied even a little
But felt she had earned the right
To wear any kind of raiment
That would enhance the glow
Of the best of all theaters,
Known as Mollie Bailey's Show.

## EPILOGUE

Following their mother's death the four boys attempted to carry on the show. Mollie, however, had given her sons little responsibility and they were not able to handle the task without her guiding hand. Eugene managed first but his health failed and Brad, who followed, died in the influenza epidemic of 1919. Allie and William Kirkland dissolved the circus in the early 1920's and started a motor truck moving picture show that played in Louisiana and Mississippi. When W. K. died in the mid-1920's, the last surviving son, Allie, settled in Louisiana. Thus, the curtain came down on a great family of entertainers, the "Bailey Family Troupe."

# Miriam Amanda Ferguson

MIRIAM FERGUSON

# Miriam Amanda Ferguson

by
BILLY M. JONES

Miriam Amanda Wallace Ferguson was a remarkable woman, a person unique in Texas history because of her unprecedented accomplishment: she was the first and, to date, only female to be elected governor of Texas. Even more remarkable is the fact that her accomplishments might never have become a reality had not her husband, James Edward Ferguson, been impeached and removed from that office. Thus the story of Mrs. Ferguson's career cannot be told without relating, almost paragraph by paragraph, the story of her husband's political career.

Almost every observer wishing to relate the Ferguson Years has faced the problem. Her daughter, Ouida Ferguson Nalle, entitled her reminiscences, *The Fergusons of Texas: Two Governors for the Price of One*. James Thomas DeShields dealt with them as *The Fergusons, "Jim and Ma," the Stormy Petrels in Texas Politics.* And most recently Professor Jack Lynn Calbert has treated them as *James Edward and Miriam Amanda Ferguson: The "Ma" and "Pa" of Texas Politics.* Their careers were truly as inseparable as were their personal lives together. A remarkable couple indeed! And they more or less dominated politics in Texas for almost three decades — at least they were the most talked about actors on the Texas political stage from 1914 to 1940. What follows is but a summary of their fascinating lives and political careers, told as exclusively from Miriam's side as is possible.

Miriam was a native Texan, born to sturdy pioneer parents in Bell County. Her father, Joseph Lapsly Wallace, followed the normal pattern of early settlers, becoming a hard working and ultimately a highly successful farmer and stockman. His industry was not unusual, for it came undoubtedly from a long and noble ancestry dating to the days of King Edward I of England. One brave warrior who fought successfully against that monarch was a Scotch patriot, Sir William Wallace, a nobleman to whom Joseph Lapsley, and thus Miriam Amanda, could trace lineal ancestry.

Joe Wallace was born in Kentucky on July 11, 1833, and came to Texas with his parents during the last days of the Texas Republic. They settled on the banks of Little River in Bell County, about seven miles from Belton. Joe served in the Confederate Army and returned to the family farm at the close of the war. In 1869, he married Eliza Garrison Ferguson, widow of Wesley Ferguson. (Wesley was an uncle of James E. Ferguson to whom Miriam would be married in 1899.) Joe Wallace raised his family in a pioneer community. He was of a "steady God-fearing stock, the type that is the backbone of any nation." And he loved and indulged his children, especially, as his fortune continued to grow. He gave his children such education as was then available. Miriam was first tutored at home, later attended a log-cabin school in Salado where she made good grades, and then completed her education at Baylor Female College in Belton in 1898.

By then Miriam had grown to womanhood. She was, even by standards in the late nineteenth century, pretty and attractive with a wealth of curly brown hair. It was stylish to be plump, and counting calories was not the mania it has become today. But plump Miriam was not, at least not to the extent she felt would make her fashionable, and she was obliged to cover "her flat bust and slender hips" with "a few ruffles in the front, and a little padding in the rear." But her cousin by marriage (there was no blood relationship), James E. Ferguson, thought her to be a handsome woman and fell in love at first sight with "the little curly headed girl four years his junior."

Miriam and James were more or less thrown together by circumstances. Her father, Joe Wallace, had taken a shipment of cattle to Kansas City during the winter of 1898, unfortunately overexposed himself during the train ride, and became seriously ill by the time he returned home. He died shortly thereafter, but left his family a small fortune in cash, bank stock, land, and cotton gins. Since Mr. Wallace's nephew, James Ferguson, was a lawyer, it was only natural that Mrs. Wallace would turn to him for legal advice. In the months that followed, James and Miriam saw each other frequently, always properly, and always with James relentlessly pursuing a reluctant Miriam. Finally after several months of persistance, Jim took her as his bride on December 31, 1899. He was twenty-eight; she was twenty-four.

Jim knew the prize he had won. He was born to poverty and knew it at every turn until his early adulthood. He left home at the age of sixteen to work at odd jobs in the West, but returned to Bell County two years later. He read law, passed the bar exam in 1897 and began his practice in Belton just in time to become counselor to the Wallaces, and to begin his quest for fair Miriam's hand.

It was a good marriage. Soon Ouida was born, and then a second daughter, Ruby Dorrace arrived. And Jim launched out into banking. He rapidly became a successful businessman, and Miriam seemed well pleased with her role as housewife and mother. The years between 1899 and 1914 apparently were happy ones.

But the gubernatorial bee was buzzing around Jim's hat band, a political urge that derived from no prior experience or declared inclination. And he was hardly known outside the county in which he lived, nor was he college trained. He was wealthy, however, in his own right and perceptive enough to recognize the issues of his era.

Texas was, in 1914, predominately a rural state. Tenant farmers were chafing under oppressive sharecropping fees imposed by landowners, and farmers' income in general was dismally low. Other issues — prohibition, education, the prison system, high railroad and warehousing rates — were volatile also, and Jim Ferguson set out to adapt his platform on these issues to an interpretation which the average farmer might make. He soon became known as "Farmer Jim," and though he spoke polished English in polite company, he made a fetish of rolling up his sleeves and firing rough language at those "city slickers" and "educated fools." His rural audiences loved him; he spoke their language.

And they elected him despite the opposition of powerful politicians such as President Woodrow Wilson, Secretary of State William Jennings Bryan and Senator Joseph Bailey of Texas. Ferguson defeated Thomas H. Ball, "a lawyer who served railroad interests," in the July Democratic Primary, and swept to victory in the November general elections. The tenant issue had done it.

Thus Miriam Amanda Wallace Ferguson, who scarcely had journeyed very far beyond Belton or Temple in her whole life, moved with her victorious husband to the governor's mansion. For her the change was not dramatic, for she had been "reared in an atmosphere of culture." She entertained with grace and dignity on the many occasions when her husband's social life dictated. But in her quieter moments she was a loving wife and mother, and maintained a home of simple and uncomplicated regimen. Her favorite personal past-time was puttering around in a flower garden and in the greenhouse she had built in 1915. She was seldom criticized in her role as first lady, though one opportunist denounced her for hiring a secretary.

Although Miriam's life was as normal as any governor's wife's could be, she was increasingly aware that all was not well in her husband's political life. As election year 1916 approached, Farmer Jim's opponents seemingly were legion. He had offended prominent businessmen, university officials and party leaders. There were rumors of his mishandling of state funds, improper placement of state revenues in certain banks, and acceptance of an unsecured and non-repayment loan from powerful lobby interests.

Standing for reelection in 1916, Governor Ferguson was opposed by Charles H. Morris, a man who attempted to out-Ferguson, Jim Ferguson himself in his emotional and political appeal to voters. He was, in Morris's own words: "a plain businessman who knows nothing about politics; . . . a man who never swore an oath . . .. who does not know one card from another . . . who knows no dance, and has never been in a ballroom in his life." Shades of Farmer Jim and his campaign oratory in 1914!

Apparently the emerging rumors were without effect, and Morris could find nothing but his "me-too" pitch on which to base his efforts. Ferguson won the July primary handily as well as the November general election. He began what seemed to be a quiet second term.

But his continuing verbal battle with university officials only served to increase the determination of his other critics to get at the root of the rumors and oust him from office. So it was that almost from the start of his second term, James E. Ferguson began a fight for his political life, a fight he lost at every turn. Impeachment in the House of Representatives, conviction in the Senate, removal from the office of governor, and ultimately a sustaining court decision on June 12, 1924, were events which were to prove quite fateful to the political career of Ferguson and to the history of Texas.

June 12, 1924, should have been a disheartening day for former governor James Edward Ferguson: the Texas Supreme Court declared that he was ineligible to hold any elective office in the State. To a great extent, it was disheartening, but the verdict was not totally unanticipated. Almost seven years earlier, on September 25, 1917, the Texas Senate had decreed similarly:

> Now, therefore, it is adjudged by the Senate of the State of Texas sitting as a Court of Impeachment, at their chamber, in the city of Austin, that the said James E. Ferguson be and he is hereby removed from the office of Governor and be disqualified to hold any office of honor, trust or profit under the State of Texas.

From that decree on September 25, 1917, until the ruling on June 12, 1924, Ferguson never ceased his maneuvering, valiantly and almost desperately seeking to keep his political career alive by running unsuccessfully for various national offices. Finally on May 1, 1924, he openly challenged the Senate decree by announcing his candidacy for governor. In a matter of less than six weeks, he was ordered to end his candidacy.

Disheartened? Undoubtedly — but not defeated. He had a following among Texas voters of proven loyalty. Twice they had elected him to the governor's chair, first in 1914 and again in 1916. And he knew only too well that many of his followers were still faithful, for he had come close to victory in 1922 in his quest for a seat in the United States Senate.

Disheartened but definitely not defeated, Jim surprised many Texans by announcing that his wife, Miriam Amanda Wallace Ferguson, would run for the governorship in his place. Declaring that "the people shall have a chance to vote for a Ferguson on a Ferguson platform," he concluded that there was no need "to quibble over first names." Ferguson filed her name as a candidate and the Democratic Executive Committee, which earlier had contested his own candidacy, promptly certified Miriam's eligibility.

Female suffrage was relatively new in Texas, and full legal equality for women still was many years in the future. Moreover, no woman had ever been elected to the office of governor in any state! Many politicians had given lipservice to the need for suffrage and equality for females — now an undaunted Jim Ferguson would give them an opportunity to demonstrate the sincerity of their words.

Miriam's first public announcement seemed much too timid, definitely not in the bold, fiery temperament of James Edward Ferguson, the poverty-to-riches champion of the Texas farmer and wage earner. She admitted an almost total lack of prior interest in politics, that she had voted but few times, and that "most of her life had been spent in home affairs and in the rearing of her children." But she had a purpose for making the race: she wanted to see her husband vindicated of the impeachment decree which the Senate had imposed on him, an action which "had brought great shame and punishment" to the entire Ferguson family. As Professor Calbert has written, she would lay upon the altar of public opinion the true decision as to Ferguson's guilt or innocence. To some observers, her task and Jim's problems seemed impossible.

In his three short years as governor, Ferguson may have won the hearts of a majority of Texas voters, but he had incurred the wrath of powerful interest groups in state politics. His easy maneuverings left some question as to his honesty in handling state funds, especially in the propriety of placing such monies on deposit in banks in which he had vested interests. Then, when he quarreled bitterly with University of Texas officials over school appropriations and faculty workloads, he became ensnarled in a controversy which apparently sealed his fate. At least Ferguson believed that friends of the University led the fight to bring impeachment charges against him.

The charges, twenty-one in all, were raised in the Texas House of Representatives in August, 1917, charges ranging from improper "financial transactions, to the [unlawful] expenditure of funds appropriated . . . for the maintenance of the Governor's mansion, the veto of the University [of Texas] appropriation, the removal of members of the board of University regents . . ." and to other similar or related matters. The Senate vote was 26-4 with one senator absent and not voting; overwhelmingly guilty as charged!

Thus on June 12, 1924, the Texas Supreme Court had echoed its approval of the Senate decree. But to relentless Jim Ferguson this simply meant a change in strategy; as he had said, there was no need to quibble over first names — if God's in his heaven, and a Ferguson is in the Governor's Mansion, all's bound to be right with Texas. At least that was Jim Ferguson's reasoning.

But a woman candidate for governor? Would Texas really elect a woman governor? At least one person, Charles M. Dickson of San Antonio, published a political tract on August 28, 1924, raising serious doubts about the legality of a woman serving in that high office. The answer to those doubts, as well as to James Ferguson's guilt, were to be left to "the will of the people," Texas's highest and only trustworthy tribunal."

And what of her credentials? Had she not admitted already to an almost total lack of interest in politics? Her admission certainly seems to have been true, although she could not have gone through the previous seven years of tension, frustation and bitterness — from her husband's impeachment to the announcement of her candidacy — without gaining some experience in the workings of Texas politics. Her strongest ally was her husband, a man now wise in political campaigning, and it was Jim Ferguson who launched her campaign with vigor. He did more traveling and speaking than did she, but Mrs. Ferguson frequently joined him and was quite effective in her own way. Her daughter recalls their joint campaigning thusly:

> "Mama would speak first, and in her own way ask the mothers, sisters and wives of Texas to help her clear her family's name. That was her trump card and she played it with finesse. Had she been a militant suffragist all her life, her appeal would not have had half the force it had coming from a quiet, home-loving wife and grandmother. In the name of her grandson, not in her own, she would plead and would end with: "A vote for me is a vote of confidence for my husband, who cannot be a candidate because his enemies have succeeded in barring him from holding public office."

This entreaty from a gentle woman was becoming a problem to the professional politicians; they did not know how to meet the attack, so simple and unprecedented. It had never occurred before in American politics.

Mrs. Ferguson ran on a platform of "Fergusonism" — her husband's platform — which called for a general reduction in state expenditures, sound administration for penitentiaries, more aid to common schools and less to "high brow" institutions, a general lowering of taxes, stricter regulations on interest rates, an end to some forms of prohibition legislation, and an "antimask law for the Ku Klux Klan." Naturally Jim was the chief spokesman for the platform, and she allowed him complete freedom in explaining and defending it. And in his usual style, he would "blast the opposition" and end his addresses by reminding the crowds that "a vote for Mrs. Ferguson meant two governors for the price of one," obviously referring to the fact that he intended to be fully active should she be elected.

Mrs. Ferguson always presented a picture of propriety in her campaigning. She attempted at times to play down if not excuse her husband's fiery oratory by saying that she hoped people were not overly upset by his verbal attacks on his enemies. He was, after all, of Scotch-Irish ancestry, and his temper might easily be understandable because of it. Much support came to her for her stable, kind hearted and tolerant attitudes, and especially for such well publicized gestures as openly requesting of Governor Pat Neff that he grant mercy to a "father of five," whose family was starving while he served time in the penitentiary for bootlegging.

Nothing helped her more in the 1924 campaign than the gift of a folksy nickname one that has become an indelible trademark through the years. It seems that Frank Gibler one evening was struggling to put her name into a headline in his newspaper, the Houston *Press*, and he was frustrated by his inability to fit her name into the number of spaces allotted. "Mrs. Ferguson," he claimed, left no room for anything else in the headline. "What's her first name?" he asked. "Miriam Amanda," was the reply. "M. A. . . .," he mused; "We'll call her Ma!" Gibler's pseudonym was the greatest single boost she received in her campaign. She immediately became "Ma" to almost all Texans; moreover, the "Farmer Jim" nickname of a previous era gave away to "Pa." Now they were Ma and Pa Ferguson to the voting public, but not to everyone, especially not within the family. She would not permit her children to use it, because it "just did not fit her dignity."

Ma and Pa (mostly Pa) campaigned vigorously against several Democrats in the July 1924 primary. And even though Ma was becoming increasingly a household word, she trailed Judge Felix D. Robertson 146,424 to 193,508. Lynch Davidson ran third with 141, 208. Both of the Fergusons regarded her second place finish as a major coup. She now had to be regarded as a serious candidate, and she was one step nearer the governorship. At a press conference at her home in Temple, she and Pa hardly could contain their enthusiasm. She posed for pictures in the role of a domestic housewife while making preserves, sweeping the back step, and tending farm animals. One such photograph was fortuitous: she posed in a sunbonnet. The sunbonnet was quickly grasped as a campaign symbol and she adopted "Put On Your Old Gray Bonnet" as a campaign song for the August primary runoff. Everywhere women supporters donned their bonnets as an endorsement of her candidacy.

The bonnet also cleverly symbolized her attack on Judge Felix D. Robertson. He had been endorsed by a varity of organizations, one of which proved to be his nemesis: the Ku Klux Klan. Wildly popular among some Texans during the post WWI era, much of the enthusiasm for the Klan had waned. Indeed, suspicion among many had caused the Klan by August 1924 to be the most controversial topic in Texas. Robertson, either from bad advice or from honest conviction, overrated the importance of Klan endorsement: " I am the man the Ku Klux Klan endorsed . . . And I am proud of it. I don't care whether it suits the Pope in Rome or not. I am carrying the banner of white supremacy, . . . and for America for Americans, and the rule of the white man from Washington to the school board." For many, Robertson was depicted as a candidate in a white hood. The August primary became a race between "the sunbonnet and the hood" or, at least, one between "a petticoat and a bedsheet." Fortunately for Pa, his past record was pressed into the distant background and never became a serious issue.

Robertson seemed to do well at times owing largely to the Fergusons' public pronouncements in favor of tolerance for Catholics and Jews (whom the Klan denounced) and Pa's assertion that prohibition was a failure and a corruptor of public morals, an assertion which hurt his wife's candidacy with protestant, fundamentalist preachers (who were vehement anti-liquor advocates). But Robertson and the Klan simply could not make their "Jew, Jug and Jesuit" chant ring with any dramatic effect. Time seemed to have mitigated much of the earlier foreign mania which had permeated Klan activities, and prohibition was a legal fact regardless of Pa's personal opinions. Most of the "respectable people of Texas" were won over to Miriam's camp.

Mrs. Ferguson beat Felix Robertson by almost 100,000 votes in the August primary. She declared her victory as a judgment against the invisible and insidious empire of Ku Klux Klan, and the Texas and national presses hailed her nomination as a vindication of the cause of popular government. Front page headlines in the New York *Times* and editorials in numerous papers across the nation heralded the triumph as a "victory over the powers of darkness and bigoted intolerance," and declared that politics would now "test the qualities of women just as it had men."

All of this could have turned Miriam's head. But she could not bask too long in the sunlight of partial success. There was a November opponent to fight, a family name to vindicate, and a state to be governed if she could win in the general election. She did not change her folksy ways in making her November bid against Republican George C. Butte; she maintained herself in ordinary rural garb and coaxed newsmen to photograph her tending chickens, working with her daughters in the cotton fields, peeling peaches in the kitchen, or swinging in the front porch swing. She was and would continue to be just "plain old Ma Ferguson."

George Butte, a former law professor at the University of Texas whom Ferguson had attacked in 1917, ran an intelligent race but was swamped by another Ferguson landslide. Even then Butte pulled more votes than had any previous Republican for the governorship. And the Klan, in a last ditch stand, sounded its own death knell by supporting Butte.

Now, Ma Ferguson was governor. Or was she? Critics regarded her merely as the window dressing; the real governor, in everything but name, was old Farmer Jim. He "merely dominated the executive office from the bedroom." Evidence seems strongly to support this thesis. He received an appointment to the all important Highway Commission and dispensed contracts, it was alleged, only to favored firms. Moreover, he "persuaded" Ma to pardon, furlough, parole, and otherwise free some 2000 inmates of the state prisons — sometimes even before they began to serve their sentences. The governor openly admitted that "her husband made these decisions."

Ferguson defended this liberal pardoning policy on grounds of economy in state government. His opponents accused him of selling or otherwise profiting from it. One remarkable two page pamphlet, published anonymously, reproduced two public documents, one the signed, voluntary confession of a William H. Langhorn, Jr., who had been sentenced to death for rape and murder. The other was a deed of trust lien, signed by Langhorn, from the records of Washington County, Texas, describing more than two thousand acres of land which was conveyed in trust to secure six promissory notes to James E. Ferguson and T. H. McGregor, Jim's longtime friend and political ally. The pamphlet concluded with the statement that by order of Governor Miriam A. Ferguson, Langhorn's sentence was commuted.

Ma seemed not to be disturbed by such charges, and she made only half hearted attempts to persuade the legislature to effect greater economics in government, to enact stronger laws against bootlegging, and to raise gasoline taxes for highway improvements and tobacco taxes for school financing. Responses to her pleas were even less enthusiastic, although the legislature did pass, and she signed into a law, a measure to "unmask the Klan." The new law made illegal the wearing of the traditional Klan regalia in public parks and thoroughfares, but by the time it took effect the Klan had virtually suspended all its activities.

Perhaps the most amusing controversy of Mrs. Ferguson's administration involved a dispute with wealthy Amon G. Carter, publisher of the Fort Worth *Star Telegram*. Carter was chairman of the Board of Directors of the newly established Texas Technological College in Lubbock, and he was a known imbiber. She had vowed to punish the rich imbibers, those "liquor-loving, scandal-mongering, privilege-mad" rich who seemed always to escape punishment while the poor were jailed for possession of a single pint of illegal booze. Moreover, Ma asserted, any college kid caught with liquor would be suspended from school; why shouldn't a Board Chairman abide by the same rules. Ma demanded Carter's resignation when she learned that he had been "drunk as a biled owl" at a Texas-Texas A & M football game. Carter branded the claim as a malicious lie, and refused to resign.

About her social life and personal habits while governor, Professor Calbert records this brief summary: Mrs. Ferguson did not cut a wide social swath as governor. She made few speeches, and a few social functions were held at the mansion. She on occasion received well-known personalities such as Will Rogers . . . .

Her public life was not unlike that of any other governor, except for one prominent fact: her "advisor and confidant" set up his desk besides her's. She always got to the office early, but she also left early, at about three o'clock each afternoon. Mr. Ferguson kept the office open until six o'clock each day while "Ma" drove around Austin or tended her chickens. Pa busied himself with office routine, planning the governor's work and visiting with legislators who dropped by for consultation. He laughed off comments about him being the real governor, and if indeed he was not, his deriders probably came close to giving him his proper title — Prince Consort or Prime Minister. But then Mrs. Ferguson asserted in his defense that "any governor needed help on the job." It was obvious to everyone that Ma was getting a lot of help from Pa.

The kindest thing one can say about her first term in office is that it was conservative. Very little legislation of importance was passed; however, one bill which she signed into law unquestionally gave her immense satisfaction. After considerable debate in the House and Senate, and over the serious objection of Attorney General Daniel Moody who regarded the measure as unconstitutional, an amnesty bill was passed in 1925 which restored James Ferguson's full political rights. That the Texas constitution declared anyone who was impeached as being unfit to hold public office was undeniable, but this issue was sidestepped and was not contested in the courts for several years. In the *Ferguson Forum*, Mrs. Ferguson wrote that she was overjoyed that at last, after seven years of fighting, her husband's name had been vindicated.

The *Forum* was Jim Ferguson's braintrust, a newspaper he founded on November 8, 1917, as a political instrument to attack other newspapers which had "submarined the truth" about him during the impeachment. It was in continuous publication until April 11, 1935, and both Pa and Ma used its weekly pages to sound off on issues, opponents and emotions. Throughout her first term in office, Mrs. Ferguson issued a syndicated column which was also published in the *Forum*. In all likelihood it was ghost written by her press secretary most of the time, but it bore Ma's indelible trademarks. She was, in most cases, an early day version of Ann Landers, giving out advise on any number of subjects. Favorite topics ranged from how to avoid the divorce courts, to advice on how to rear children and keep them in school. Women should take care of their homes first, she declared — but then, she left no doubt in her personal life that she believed what she wrote. Her family always came first.

Politically, Mrs. Ferguson at first was not as controversial as her husband. She responded to the various issues of the times with the same philosophy as did most Texans. She avoided fighting with University officials in the early days. Indeed, one of the officials present at the signing of the amnesty bill was the president of the University of Texas. But eventually her policies of pardoning and highway construction caused quite a stir.

It was the latter issue that produced the chief issue on which the 1926 election was decided. Automobile travel was increasing rapidly in the twenties, and the Federal Highway Act of 1916 made money available on a matching basis to every state in the union. Through the sale of bonds Texas combined its federal grants into a fairly extensive road building project. Of course, James Ferguson sat on the Highway Commission, and the charges of favoritism in his awarding of construction contracts inevitably brought controversy and a lawsuit by Attorney General Moody. Although Moody won the case and was able to cancel a big contract with the American Road Company, he was never able to trace any wrong doing or graft to any member of the Ferguson family.

But because of the bad publicity given the entire construction contract controversy, too many people were willing to believe that there was improper conduct going on in the highway program. A serious threat to impeach Mrs. Ferguson for this and her liberal pardoning policies was thwarted by, among other reasons, her refusal to call a special session for that purpose. When legislative leaders then threatened to call a special session on their own, even to finance it through private sources, she dared them to do so, saying that they would find out how dumb and delicate she was.

No call was issued and the furor eventually died down. But a noticeable change came over the governor's office. Absent and silent was Jim Ferguson, and rumor had it that she would not seek reelection. She did keep people guessing until March 1926, when she announced her candidacy.

Her campaign was spirited but doomed from the start. Attorney General Dan Moody virtually ignored her and centered his attacks on Mr. Ferguson. This she claimed was blatant sex discrimination and further evidence that Moody's favorite passtime was that of harrassing the Fergusons. Desperately, she issued a challenge: if he led her by as much as one vote in the July primary, then she would resign from office immediately. On the other hand he should agree to resign the race if she led him by 25,000 votes. The challenge was accepted, but nothing either of the Fergusons did thereafter could stave off "a stinging rebuke." Moody won the July 24 primary by a plurality of over 100,000 votes, but Mrs. Ferguson refused to resign either her position or the race. Moody had, however, built up too great a momentum, and he swamped her in the August primary by over 200,000 votes. Even then the insult was not yet over.

A special session of the legislature called in September to consider the validation of road bonds also allowed the legislature to "investigate any department of the government" it wished. After some debate, the House decided to investigate the Highway Department and produced some damning charges against Jim: kickbacks on all contracts, bribing certain officials to cover up poor quality of work, profit sharing and even outright ownership of one company which did business with the state. Naturally Jim denied the charges.

Claims against Mrs. Ferguson's pardoning practices were almost as bad, chief among them being that clemencies were sold outright and that murderers were thus released again to endanger peace loving Texans. Embittered by these charges, especially since she had greatly reduced the number of pardons in 1926, Miriam spent her last month in office in living up to her reputation as "one of the pardoningest governors in Texas history." At Christmas time alone she freed over 150 inmates, and in the very last weeks she found sufficient justification to free "33 rapists, 133 murderers, 124 robbers, and 127 liquor law violators." Ma went out in a blaze of questionable glory.

Both of the Fergusons remained active politically from 1927 to 1930, but usually supported the losing candidates. The sores left by the last years of Ma's term caused some of Pa's enemies to seek to repeal the amnesty bill which had restored his political rights. The movement failed and Ferguson believed this to mean that he was free to run for governor again. He announced his candidacy in February 1930, was refused certification by the Democratic Executive Committee, and lost a law suit which would have forced the Committee to place his name on the primary ballot. Indeed, he lost much more. The Texas Supreme Court declared the amnesty bill to be unconstitutional. He could never hold public office again in Texas.

Out of retirement bolted "that woman" again, Mrs. Ferguson announcing her own candidacy once the decision was made final. Ross Sterling, former highway commissioner, was her principal opponent. The issues and charges sounded like broken phonograph records. Ferguson was enraged, and he labeled the ruling on the amnesty bill as "the partisoned decision of a group of judges appointed by Governor Moody." Mrs. Ferguson contended that she would have been reelected in 1926 had it not been for the fact that certain demagogues had spread falsehoods and malicious lies about her policies. Sterling countered by stating much of Texas' financial difficulties could be traced to the mismanagement of the Ferguson regime.

Financial woes were not confined to Texas, for the Great Depression had set in all across the United States. The campaign of 1930 thus centered around a single theme: which of the candidates most likely could restore prosperity in the state. Sterling's proposal that the state sell a large bond issue to build additional highways, a move calculated to raise employment levels, brought angry accusations from Jim Ferguson. Sterling, he said, was seeking only to aid his wealthy "road hog" friends in the trucking and bussing industries. Apparently Texas voters accepted Pa's interpretations because Ma won a plurality in the July 1930 primary by some 60,000 votes — but the Fergusons knew only too well that the margin in the four-candidate race left little room for rejoicing. They predicted the second primary would be difficult, and it was. Despite all efforts to brand Sterling as the kingpin for corporate wealth in Texas, and to depict Fergusonism as the movement of the common people of Texas, time and political realignments took their toll. Mrs. Ferguson lost the August primary 473,371 to 384,402. The county folk of Texas were no longer able to carry an election without a substantial city vote. And in this election, the cities voted overwhelmingly for Sterling.

Sterling had won no great prize; the depression years were at their worst between 1931 and 1933. State expenditures were of necessity very high and unemployment was staggering. When Sterling lost his own fortune in the collapse of business, he lost heart himself and became almost ineffective as governor. Little wonder that Texans began to look for change — or that the Fergusons began to reassess their political fortunes.

In February 1932, Ma announced that she would again seek the governorship, stating that she would reduce taxes across the board if she were elected. Everyone simple would have to get by with less. Taxpayers themselves were doing so; why should not state government? Moreover she pledged to encourage legislation which would assure homeowners that they would not lose their homes. And her husband used the *Forum* as a vehicle to spread the word: the depression was Republican in origin, and the Democratic "fat cats" who had profited from Hoover politics should be turned out of office. And of course this included Sterling, a person known to have business and banking ties in several Texas cities. He pointed to Sterling's support of high interest rates, his squandering of state monies on unnecessary highways along the Coast, and his enforcement of oil production controls in East Texas with Texas Rangers and the National Guard.

Sterling was more a casualty of the depression than from Ferguson's biting broadsides. Mrs. Ferguson won the first primary handily and the August runoff by a very narrow margin of 3,789 votes. Sterling was incensed, and in a called session of the legislature demanded that the election returns be investigated. This the legislature declined to do. Then Sterling filed suit claiming that illegal votes from neighboring states were recorded and that many who had not paid their poll taxes had also voted illegally. Meanwhile Mrs. Ferguson brought suit in the Texas Supreme Court to have the Democratic Executive Committee certify the vote and her nomination.

Again Sterling lost; Ma was declared the official nominee of the Democratic Party.

Sterling refused to accept her nomination and fought to have the Texas Democratic Convention repudiate her, but his efforts were fruitless. Flaming mad, he asserted that he would support the Republican ticket (which came as no surprise to Jim Ferguson, of course) and called upon "somebody to shoot Ferguson in the foot, so as to end the threat he presented to Texas politicians every two years." Despite the tirade and his defection to the opposing party, Mrs. Ferguson began her second term in 1933 after she had soundly trounced Orville Bullington, her Republican opponent in the November general elections.

Her second term was most unlike the peaceful flower garden she loved so much. The state's financial status was grave. A deficit of some fourteen million had been accumulated, and when the Security Trust Company of Austin was forced to close its doors, the state's cash deposits were wiped out. Out of necessity, state warrants had to be discounted, and the interest on state bonds was declared in default. Facing near bankruptcy, the legislature moved quickly to reduce the salaries of state employees, and even to eliminate whole departments for purposes of economy. Every possible step was taken to put the state on a balanced budget. And to avoid an even greater disaster, she ordered on March 3, 1933, the banks in Texas to close for "Texas Independence Week." They were allowed to reopen later under very strict regulations established by the Texas Legislature.

The Fergusons urged Texans to tighten their belts during the economic crisis, to develop gardens, and to quit spending their money outside of Texas. They declared all-out support for Franklin D. Roosevelt's policies, calling him "the greatest human hearted president this nation has ever had." And as FDR's New Deal made federal relief available, the Fergusons eagerly sought whatever division of funds to which Texas was entitled. Like most state executives, Mrs. Ferguson looked more to national rather than state sources for ways to mitigate the effects of the economic collapse. Funds from a variety of federal programs — FERA, CCC, NYA, WPA and others — provided relief and temporary employment for approximately one fourth of the Texas population during Mrs. Ferguson's second term.

The older issues in Texas, highway construction and pardoning, were less volatile after 1933 than before, and Texans also quickly joined the movement in 1933 to ratify the Constitutional Amendment removing the prohibition on liquor. The big issue confronting the Fergusons was how to regulate a booming oil industry. Because of new discoveries in East Texas and almost unregulated production, the market was glutted with oil. The producers of this valuable natural resource now faced the plight of the cotton farmer in the 1890's — rapidly declining prices because of oversupply.

The problem had first confronted Governor Sterling, who persuaded the legislature to pass an act giving the Railroad Commission the power to set and enforce a proration policy. However, little or no attempt had been made to enforce the law when Mrs. Ferguson started her second term.

At her insistence, and partly as a result of a need for revenue, the legislature responded by levying a tax of two cents per barrel, but failed to enact a definitive proration law. Later however, a stronger law was passed, placing all oil refineries under the regulating authority of the Railroad Commission and making all violations of proration laws a felony. Though the law left much to be desired, it was the beginning of effective regulations of the oil industry in Texas and of a much needed policy for the conservation of natural resources.

With the end of her second term approaching, Mrs. Ferguson ended all speculation about her future intentions. She would not be a candidate in the 1934 election. Her family had resided almost seven years in the governor's mansion, a period she felt was "enough honor for one family." She and her husband would continue to be interested in politics "but not office."

Thus an era ended. Mrs. Ferguson did make a last race for the governorship in 1940, but by then, the flame of Fergusonism had gone out. Even Farmer Jim had lost his zest; his *Forum* had been buried by the depression, and his advancing age left him weary after lengthy trips. He was but a shadow of the effective campaigner he was a decade earlier.

Miriam's second administration removed much of the cloud that had hovered almost constantly over the Ferguson name since the Senate's decree of impeachment in 1917. People everywhere spoke favorably of her accomplishments, particularly in the area of state economy. The absence of any type of sensationalism, or even modest rumors of scandal, speaks highly of her conduct as well as Jim's. It might also suggest that much of the early criticism was more politically motivated than substantively founded. And in marked contrast to earlier years, Miriam chose not to run again in 1934 when conditions seemed most favorable for her reelection. But, as she said, seven years was honor enough.

Ma and Pa Ferguson retired to private life after the inauguration of James V. Allred in January, 1935. Unlike Ross Sterling, who refused to attend Mrs. Ferguson's installation in 1933, Ma was present to wish the new governor godspeed. For the Fergusons, their retirement was not all peaceful. The depression had taken its toll on their modest wealth. A mortgage forclosure cost them Mrs. Ferguson's six hundred acre ranch in Bell County, and the Internal Revenue Service demanded and received payment on several thousands of dollars in back taxes. Finally, the *Forum* found few advertisers in the depression years, and Ferguson interrupted its continuous publication in April 1935, and then was finally obliged to permanently suspend its publication in July 1936. There was no serious attempt to revive it during Ma's bid for the governorship in 1940.

James E. Ferguson lived only a few years after their last attempt at the governorship. He died at the age of seventy-three on September 21, 1944, and was buried in the State Cemetery in Austin. Mrs. Ferguson, in retirement, lived quietly at her home in Austin on Windsor Road. Gardening remained her chief hobby, but she never lost her interest in politics. Only on rare occasions did she become active in campaigning for anyone, one notable exception being that of Lyndon Baines Johnson's bid for a congressional seat. Her support of Johnson continued through the Kennedy-Johnson presidential campaign in 1960.

In her later years she compiled a list of accomplishments of the Ferguson era, citing aid to "education, mental health, welfare, and the improvement of working conditions for laboring people." These she regarded as being progressive enough to brand the Fergusons as liberals. And they were common folk. They avoided any demonstration of conspicuous consumption, lived modestly, and "always rode in open Model T's when campaigning since Pa thought sedans looked plutocratic."

It is impossible to estimate the influence that Jim had on Mrs. Ferguson as governor, but it was undoubtedly very great. That she was capable of handling the office, no one could doubt, but she had such great faith in her husband that she welcomed his influence and contributions at all times.

Mrs. Ferguson passed away on June 25, 1961, in Austin at the age of eighty-six, but not before she was accorded a few honors in her own right. On Mother's Day, 1953, the Texas Senate honored her with a special resolution, citing her as "an example of noble and gentle womanhood, an ideal wife, and a devoted mother." Then on her eightieth birthday, she was honored at a banquet in the Driskill Hotel in Austin by over three hundred people, one of whom was a grateful Lyndon Baines Johnson. As a touching tribute, those present sang a memorable song for her: "Put on Your Old Gray Bonnet," her campaign song in 1924.

Descriptions of Mrs. Ferguson are numerous, but no one has left a better word picture than the one recorded by James Thomas DeShields:

> Mrs. Ferguson is a model mother and housewife. She is a tall, slender woman with flashing black eyes and tiny laugh-wrinkles around her eyes, that prove she is not void of humor. She has a peculiar habit of looking at the back of people's heads to judge their character or refresh her memory in regard to an old acquaintance. She is passionately fond of flowers and of art and music, and is more of a domestic than of a social disposition. She has moral ideals; and for one thing during the nearly half a dozen years that she presided as the mistress at the Mansion and in all the social functions that were carried on, she never

> served liquor, and this met the hearty approval of Governor James E. Ferguson. Mrs. Ferguson is cultured, refined and witty and has a happy way of dispensing "courtly etiquette when required in State occasions and as hostess to the people of Texas.

Thus a remarkable woman left an indelible imprint upon Texas history, an imprint unprecedented and, for her, wholely unanticipated. The inevitable question of "why did she do it" can better be answered in her own words:

> When I am questioned as to why I wanted to be the Governor of Texas, I hardly know how to express that desire in a few words. The subject covers so much that it is difficult to crystallize into one little paragraph. To sum it up concisely; however — of course, everyone knows that my main incentive was to clear away the cloud that political hatred had draped about the honorable name of Ferguson. I wanted to right the grevious wrong which enmity had perpetrated upon my husband, James E. Ferguson, once Governor of Texas. Frankly, that was my reason of reasons for seeking office. But naturally, having been associated and allied with political life for years, I knew the needs and problems of my State, and my interest in the welfare of our Commonwealth is deep and sincere. This, I have consistently tried to prove by my actions as Governor. Being human also, I have enjoyed the distinctive honor which has been mine as Governor of Texas — and especially in having been the first woman to receive as an expression of confidence from the people, the bestowal of this sacred trust."